Elbridge Streeter Brooks

A Boy of the first Empire

Elbridge Streeter Brooks

A Boy of the first Empire

ISBN/EAN: 9783337170080

Printed in Europe, USA, Canada, Australia, Japan

Cover: Foto ©ninafisch / pixelio.de

More available books at **www.hansebooks.com**

A BOY
OF
THE FIRST EMPIRE

"THEY RECOGNIZED PHILIP, AND STOPPED TO SPEAK WITH THE CHILDREN."
(SEE PAGE 94.)

A BOY

OF

THE FIRST EMPIRE

BY

ELBRIDGE S. BROOKS

AUTHOR OF "THE CENTURY BOOK FOR YOUNG AMERICANS," ETC.

NEW YORK
THE CENTURY CO.
1913

Copyright, 1894, 1895, by
THE CENTURY CO.

CONTENTS

CHAPTER	PAGE
I. "Uncle Bibiche"	1
II. A Prince of the Sans-Culottes	10
III. The School-boy of St. Cyr	22
IV. The Ball at the Embassy	36
V. In the Street of the Fight	48
VI. A Fuss with Fouché	59
VII. The Mission of Citizen Daunou	76
VIII. The "Courier of the King"	93
IX. "That Pig of a Pierre"	107
X. The Tower of St. Jacques	121
XI. The Pupils of the Guard	134
XII. How Philip Baited the Russian Bear	147
XIII. What Mademoiselle found in the Street of St. Anthony	157
XIV. Why Philip was mad at the Clerk of the Weather	172
XV. The Prisoner of Fontainebleau	183
XVI. For France	194
XVII. Brother and Sister	208
XVIII. "The Claws of the Corsican"	221
XIX. How the Schoolboys fought at Paris	235
XX. The Fall of the Tricolor	249
XXI. The Swarming of the Bees	262
XXII. "Into the Furnace-Flame"	278
XXIII. How Philip played the Stowaway	293
XXIV. The City of Refuge	310

LIST OF ILLUSTRATIONS

	PAGE
THEY RECOGNIZED PHILIP, AND STOPPED TO SPEAK WITH THE CHILDREN .... FRONTISPIECE	
"UNCLE BIBICHE"	7
"'SEIZE THE ASSASSIN'"	12
"'COME, YOU BOY; YOU ARE TO GO WITH US,' THE POLICEMAN SAID"	19
"THE EMPEROR'S FAMOUS CHAPEAU COVERING HIS CURLY HEAD, AND THE EMPEROR'S 'SWORD OF MARENGO' TRAILING ON THE FLOOR BEHIND HIM"	25
CADET DESNOUETTES AND CORPORAL PEYROLLES.—"'BE A SOLDIER OF FRANCE!'"	31
"THE EMPRESS HELD OUT A HAND WHICH PHILIP LOYALLY KISSED"	43
PHILIP STRIKES UNCLE FAURIEL	57
"'I AM HAPPY TO BE NEAR YOU, SIRE,' SAID PHILIP"	65
UNCLE FAURIEL SHAKES HIS FIST AT FOUCHÉ	69
"'GO! YOU ARE DISMISSED FROM THE SERVICE OF THE EMPEROR!'"	74
PHILIP RIDES ON THE STEP OF THE EMPRESS'S CARRIAGE.	81
"'THERE WAS BUT THIS BOY,' THE EMPEROR SAID"	87
"'I PRESENT TO YOU THE KING OF ROME!'"	97
THE "COURIER OF THE KING"	101
"'MY FRIEND!' PHILIP CRIED, 'I OWE YOU MUCH'"	111
"'GONE!' HE GASPED"	115
"'SAVE HIM, SIRE!' SHE EXCLAIMED"	125
"THEN SHE TOLD HER STORY"	129
PHILIP'S GRATITUDE	137

LIST OF ILLUSTRATIONS

	PAGE
Napoleon reviews the Pupils of the Guard	143
Philip and the Russian Ambassador	154
"Napoleon pulled the Page's Hair vigorously in Appreciation of the Joke"	164
"'What is that, Pierre?' she said, pointing to the Words"	170
"'Stand back, sirs,' he cried. 'This is the Apartment of the Empress!'"	179
The Emperor saves Philip from the Boar	191
Napoleon's Veterans viewing the Portrait of the King of Rome	199
"'What can your Majesty make of such a Dandy?'"	203
"The Eye of the Emperor, he felt, was upon him"	217
"He showed her where a Tatar Arrow had torn an ugly Hole"	225
Philip taken Prisoner by the Cossacks	233
Philip before Marshal Blücher. The Letter is found	237
Corporal Peyrolles and the Polytechnic Boys fighting in the Defense of Paris	245
"The Emperor placed a Hand upon his Head"	257
"'Off with the Lilies — on with the Bees!'"	273
The Emperor decorates Philip with his own Cross of the Legion of Honor	276
"'Ride like the Wind to Paris. Tell them the Battle is won'"	289
"'To-morrow you may be at Sea, safe under the American Flag'"	297
"'I will punish you for this!' the enraged Marshal cried"	302
Diving down into the Hold	307

A BOY
OF
THE FIRST EMPIRE

A BOY OF THE FIRST EMPIRE

CHAPTER I

"UNCLE BIBICHE"

ON a certain June morning in the year 1806, when the sunshine flooded all things, and every nightingale in France seemed practising for the post of court singer, a boy lay at the foot of one of the great chestnuts in the park of St. Cloud.

He was small, disreputable-looking, and dilapidated,—a tramp, and a ragged little tramp at that; but his eye was bright and snappy; his tangled hair, crowned with the wreck of a red liberty-cap, was thick and golden; and his face, though it bore the stamp of poverty as it bore its crust of grime, had that careless, happy-go-lucky air that marks the street-boy of any great city.

His restless eyes took in everything the noble park had to offer. He was evidently on the lookout for some place or some person. But, tired with his ten-mile tramp, and overpowered by the glorious solitude of all out-of-doors,—burdened, also, with the weight of the important secret that had led him so far from his dingy home in the narrow Street of the Washerwomen,— he had flung himself down at the foot of the great chestnut to talk it all over with himself, for want of a listening comrade.

"My faith!" he said, as he closed one eye and squinted the other along the fat tree-trunk and into the overarching branches, "but this is n't the Court of the Miracles now, nor yet the Street of the Washerwomen, is it? What big trees! What a lot of room! Lonesome, though, I think, when the night comes down; even the Street of the Washerwomen would be better than this, for there are plenty of people there,—more than a plenty sometimes, especially when that pig of a Pierre comes shoving across the street to tease Babette and set my two fists a-going! But I like *people*. There 's more to see in a crowd of people than in a crowd of trees—more to do, too. But here 's where the Little Corporal's big house is, somewhere among these trees. I wonder where? I saw a pile of buildings on the hill farther along, as I came up here. Perhaps I can find the Emperor there. I must; I must n't say what I came for to any one else. I wonder how one talks to an emperor? Must I say 'Citizen Emperor,' or 'Citizen Little Corporal,' or 'Citizen' what? I must find out before I get up to his house. I 'll have to ask somebody. Pst! There 's some one moving through those trees. Hi, there, Citizen! No, it is n't a man; it 's a boy. No, it 's a dog; no, it 's a—my faith, though! what can it be? It 's not a dog, nor a horse, nor a pig, nor yet a—it must be a sheep—or a wolf. There 's another—and another—and more of them; and a man, too. Perhaps they are wolves—the beasts that Mother Thérèse says eat you up in the forest. Perhaps they will eat the man up. What fun! I don't want them to eat me, though. So! I'll slip behind this big tree, and see what is to be." And, suiting the action to the word, the boy, who, half raised from the ground, had been watching with wide-open eyes the moving figures, scrambled to his feet, and, sheltered behind the big chestnut, peered around the trunk, anxious to see what might be about to happen. For a boy of the Paris streets had but vague ideas as to the ways of forest life, and, though inquisitive, was cautious.

Across the open space that lay between the wide avenue and the grove of stately chestnut-trees came the figure of a man, and at his heels, sniffing and thronging, moved the creatures that were so strange and inexplicable to the peeping city-boy — a dozen of the tame Barbary antelopes of St. Cloud.

They were dainty, timorous, graceful little beasts; but desire had overcome timidity, and they trooped after the man, now crowding all about him, now starting back in alarm as he plunged his hand into his coat pocket; but at him again they charged when his hand was withdrawn, and one and then another of the antelopes would thrust a brown muzzle into the extended hand, and, with sneeze and snort, lick up the powdery offering it held.

The man was of medium height, long of body and short of legs, rather stout, but yet not fat. His age was less than forty; his face was fine and cleanly cut, though tanned by sun and weather. From his tumbled brown hair rose a plain cocked hat, set well forward on his large head. He wore a long and thin gray overcoat, and in the deep pockets lay the loose snuff, for a taste of which the thronging antelopes were nosing and pushing one another, eager for preference.

The boy behind the tree gazed intently at the curious group that passed him, forgetting his own mission in the interest it excited. Then, remembering his desire, he was about to call out "Hi, Citizen!" and ask how he could see and what he should call the Emperor, when through the trees came the shrill call of a child:

"Uncle Bibiche, Uncle Bibiche—oh, Uncle Bibiche!"

The antelopes, startled by the call, stopped their nosing and pushing, and looked back in alarm; the man with the snuff in his overcoat pocket also looked back, and his face broke into a smile of welcome.

"So, little pig; it is you, then?" he said. "Do you, too, wish the snuff? Come; come and catch us;" and he broke away in a run, followed by the trooping antelopes.

"Wait, wait, Uncle Bibiche; wait for Baby!" the little runner panted. "Baby wants a ride."

But as he hurried fast and faster after the runaways, his little foot caught in a half-exposed root; he tripped and fell, rolling down the bit of bank where rose the great chestnut-tree behind which stood the boy from Paris.

A cry of surprise that grew into the loud wail of grief broke from the sprawling one, and Uncle Bibiche turned quickly about and hurried toward him. But, before the man could reach the scene of disaster, the street-boy had darted from his hiding-place and picked up the prostrate baby.

"Hi, there, little one! Come up, come up," he said. "So; you are not hurt now, are you?" and he brushed the dirt from the fine clothes of the child.

Uncle Bibiche, too, dropped on his knees and drew an arm about the child, who, even in his grief, remembered the treat he sought. "A ride—Uncle—Bibiche, I—want—a ride," he whimpered.

"Yes, he shall have a ride, so he shall, sha'n't he, Citizen Uncle?" said the street-boy, soothingly, still brushing away the dust.

Uncle Bibiche turned a searching eye upon the speaker. "Well, boy, and how came you here? Where did you drop from?" he demanded.

"Not from the sky, Citizen Uncle," the boy replied glibly. "I am of the city."

"From the city? Then how got you here?" Uncle Bibiche asked.

The boy laughed. "Why, Citizen Uncle, with the same horses the Emperor has to carry him—Shank and Spindle;" and he slapped each stout little leg in explanation.

The man in the gray coat pulled the street-boy's tangled hair. "You 're a bold talker, you," he said. And the child, who had been peering into the dirty face of his rescuer, caught at the word "horses" and echoed them.

"Baby wants horse, too; carry Baby!" he demanded.

"Why, of course, little one; I carry babies every day," the boy responded; and, catching up the child, he began to prance and trot with him, like a mettlesome charger.

The baby laughed, and Uncle Bibiche laughed, flicking at the make-believe horse with his silk handkerchief as though it were a whip, whereupon the child repeated his demand: "Uncle Bibiche, Baby wants to ride sheep now," pointing toward the antelopes.

"So; I said they were sheep," the boy cried. "How do you ride them?"

"Uncle Bibiche knows. Let Baby ride sheep," the spoiled child clamored.

"All right, Citizen Uncle; he's yours," and the boy set the little fellow on the ground.

But the baby, grasping Uncle Bibiche's long coat with one hand, with the other clung to his new friend. "Let dirty boy go, too," he demanded.

Uncle Bibiche plunged a hand into his capacious coat pocket and drew it out, filled with snuff, seeing which action the antelopes thronged about him again. Clapping a hand upon each of the child's shoulders, Uncle Bibiche lifted the small fellow from the ground and set him astride the back of one of the antelopes.

"Steady him on the other side, you boy," said Uncle Bibiche. Then, with the street-boy holding him on one side and Uncle Bibiche on the other, the little rider laughed aloud in glee as, mounted on his queer steed, he rode along the broad, chestnut-bordered avenue of St. Cloud.

But the boy from Paris could not long keep quiet. He remembered his errand, too.

"Citizen Uncle," he said; "might one see the Emperor?"

"Yes, one might," Uncle Bibiche replied. "For example, you?"

"For example, me," the boy declared. "I have business with him."

At this Uncle Bibiche laughed loudly, whereupon the antelope-rider laughed, and the boy from Paris laughed too.

"And what might be your business with the Emperor, bold one?" Uncle Bibiche inquired.

"That is for him to know," the boy answered. "But tell

us, Citizen Uncle; what should one call him? Should one say—Citizen Emperor—or—Citizen Little Corporal—or—Citizen what?"

"UNCLE BIBICHE."

Uncle Bibiche looked across the antelope at his questioner. Then he said to the rider, who was kicking his small legs against the side of his uneasy steed, "Dirty boy wants to see the Emperor, little pig. What shall the boy call the Emperor, eh?"

"Call him Grandpapa," replied the little lad promptly, and then all three laughed gleefully again.

"But it is not to be laughed at, my business, Citizen Uncle," the boy from Paris said soberly. "It is to save the Emperor's skin."

"And from whom would you save his skin, you boy?" Uncle Bibiche inquired.

"That is our business, too—mine and the Emperor's," said the boy, earnestly.

"None may see the Emperor—on business, here—save those who tell their business before they see him," Uncle Bibiche explained. "Tell me your business, and I will get speech of the Emperor for you; for me he will sometimes hear. What would you say to him?"

The boy from Paris looked searchingly at Uncle Bibiche. Then he said: "Jacques has gone for a soldier; Pierre has gone for a soldier. They will fight for the Little Corporal, and perhaps bring back the cross as did one-legged Antoine, who lives just beyond us in the Street of Jean Lantier. Perhaps if the Emperor hears what I have to tell him, he will let me go for a soldier, too. Citizen Uncle, let me see the Emperor." Then he lowered his voice: "A plot; I know of a plot against him. I would save his life."

"A plot? You know of a plot against the Emperor, you boy? What is it? Out with it!" and the gray eyes looked sternly at the eager but ragged little petitioner on the other side of the antelope. "Do you speak truth, you boy?"

"Why should I lie?" the boy said, meeting the sharp gray eyes without flinching. "I have walked from the Street of the Washerwomen for this—not to lie to the

Emperor, Citizen Uncle, but to tell him what I know. Let me see him, then. Where is he?"

Uncle Bibiche caught the four-year-old rider from the antelope's back, and stood him on the ground.

"Attention, comrade!" he said, as if giving an order. "Who is the Emperor?"

And the little fellow, standing straight as a ramrod, brought his hand to his forehead in soldierly salute.

"Uncle Bibiche!" he said.

CHAPTER II

A PRINCE OF THE SANS-CULOTTES

THE boy from Paris fell back in astonishment. Then he laughed in nervous dismay, and then in open distrust.

"What! Citizen Uncle the Emperor? Come now, Baby, but that's a good one! Why, he's not little; he's bigger than Jacques; and they call the Emperor the *Little* Corporal; and he marches about with his guards, and wears a gold crown on his head. And this one — why, this is only just Uncle Bibiche. You're playing the fool with us, you little one, are you not, now? Come, then, if you but show me the way to the Emperor, I'll give you the song and dance with which I pay my toll over the Little Bridge, when I go to the Isle of the City." And, catching the child by both hands, the boy from Paris whirled him about, and danced him around, capering like an imp, and singing the chorus:

"Zig-zag; rig-a-doon,
So we dance to the drumstick's tune!"

It was great sport for the little four-year-old, though a trifle rough, perhaps. But he enjoyed it immensely. As for Uncle Bibiche, he laughed aloud and said, "You're a crazy one, you boy. You caper and sing like a carmagnole. Tell us, who are you?"

The boy stopped short in his mad dance, and a roguish twinkle made his eyes yet more snappy.

"I, Citizen Uncle," he said,—and here he clicked his heels together and brought his hand in salute to his shock of golden hair, just as he had seen his little playmate do,— "I am a prince of the sans-culottes!"

Uncle Bibiche made a dash at the boy's ear and pinched it in high glee. "You're a crazy one, you boy," he said again; and then he added, "So, my children! Here we have the royal family in council—two princes and an emperor. Come, tell us your grand plot."

The boy from Paris straightway became sober. "We are playing the fool too much, we three. Come, Uncle Bibiche, let me see this Emperor."

"What! do you not believe our little prince here?" Uncle Bibiche said. "Trifler! Must we prove him true?"

Then, taking a silver whistle from his pocket, he blew it loudly. Scarcely had the shrill call died away when two foresters, in a livery of green studded with golden bees, came swiftly beneath the great tree.

"Where are the guard?" Uncle Bibiche demanded.

"Within call, Sire," one of the foresters replied.

The boy from Paris started at the word, and looked sharply at the man in the gray overcoat.

"Summon them, you," Uncle Bibiche said, whereupon one of the foresters darted up the avenue, and two long whistle-signals rang out beneath the trees. A moment later, and the measured rhythm of the double-quick sounded on the hard road. Then, down the broad avenue, with a corporal in the lead, came hurrying a file of the Grenadiers of the Guard. They stopped before Uncle Bibiche and presented arms.

"'SEIZE THE ASSASSIN!'"

The boy from Paris began to feel uncomfortable. His mouth slowly opened; he shifted uneasily from one foot to the other. But he stood it pluckily, eagerly watchful.

"Corporal," said Uncle Bibiche, sharply, "is this the way to guard our park? How do suspicious characters — for example, this one,"—and he pointed an accusing finger at the boy from Paris—" get within its limits ? "

The corporal of the guard saluted. "The chief forester shall be asked, Sire," he said. " His men are not watchful. Meantime, are we to take this rascally one, Sire ? "

The boy from Paris looked steadfastly on the man in the gray overcoat. Then came the order, " Seize the assassin ! " and still the boy did not flinch.

"Assassin, Sire ? This puny one ? Has it come even to that ? " and the corporal's hand fell heavily upon the boy's shoulder. And still there came no word in denial or protest.

But protest did come from another quarter.

"Take your hands off my dirty boy ! " cried the Prince. " He picked me up; he held me on; he danced me about. I like him."

The Emperor—for such indeed was he whom the little four-year-old called " Uncle Bibiche "—Napoleon, Emperor of France, whose summer palace was in this beautiful park of St. Cloud—the Emperor smiled down upon the baby Prince. "Here is a bold champion," he said. "Come, let the boy go, Corporal. He is Prince Napoleon's prisoner, and my word to you was to try his spirit. But bid the chief forester be more watchful. Withdraw ! " and he made a movement in dismissal.

The corporal released his prisoner, saluted, and stepped back.

As he did so the little Prince Napoleon—the son of the Emperor's brother Louis, King of Holland, and his wife Hortense, daughter of the Empress Josephine — grasped the arm of the boy from Paris, stood before the grenadiers, and raised his hand in salute to the Emperor. "Long live Grandpapa!" he cried. The grenadiers presented arms, and, at the word from their corporal, wheeled about, and marched away.

"Well, my prince of the sans-culottes, how now? May I hear of your plot?" the Emperor asked.

"Citizen Sire," the boy from Paris replied, still a trifle perplexed. "I could not think you were the Little Cor— the Emperor. I would not have danced so — nor so have shaken up Prince Little One, here."

"'T was a good dance, and a healthy shaking up. Come —the plot—the plot," the Emperor said impatiently.

Thereupon in straightforward way the boy from Paris told his story: How, in Citizen Popon's wine-shop, whither he had been sent by Mother Thérèse for the washing of the Citizeness Popon, he had (while hiding in a dark corner so that he might spring out upon young Victor Popon, with whom he was at feud) overheard a conversation between three men who sat at table close by, and how these three conspirators planned to meet that next night, at the stroke of nine, on the old Tower wharf, near to where the gate used to stand, to see the man from England, who had a plan to kill the Emperor, and fill all their pockets with gold. And this, the boy said, was all he had to tell, because, just then, young Victor Popon came hunting about for him, and he had dropped quickly to the floor and crawled noiselessly from his hiding-place, for fear Victor would come upon him there, and he, then, would be set upon by the three rascally ones. And when the next morning came, he had, because he had thought over the matter all night, hastened from his home in the Street of the Washerwomen straight to St. Cloud, to find the Emperor, and tell him what he had heard; because he had no wish that the Emperor should be killed; besides, if they killed the Emperor, what chance would there be for one to enter the army, as Jacques and Pierre had done?

"And so you, too, would go for a soldier, you boy?" the Emperor demanded, when the boy's story was told.

"That would I, Citi—Sire," the boy replied. "My father was a soldier, so Mother Thérèse says—and says, too, for which I hate her, that he was an enemy of the people!— and fought for the king, before the Terror."

"An *émigré*, eh!" exclaimed the Emperor, using the word by which were denoted those who, because they belonged to the royalist party in France, were compelled to "emigrate" or leave their homeland as exiles. "And what is your name, you boy?"

"The boys of our quarter call me 'mud prince' and 'little 'ristocrat,' Sire," the boy from Paris made answer. "But I am Philip, the son of the *émigré* Desnouettes, who, in spite of the edict, came back to France when I was but a baby, and lost his head to sharp Madame Guillotine. I live with Mother Thérèse, and I tire of it all. If I am mud prince, as they call me, I am to be gold prince some day, so I tell Babette—if but the Emperor will."

"And who is Babette?"

"Oh, Babette is Mother Thérèse's little one, Sire,—the only bright thing in our Street of the Washerwomen," young Philip replied. "I have to defend her against that pig of a Pierre over the way. He is ever teasing her, and I hate boys who worry those who cannot strike back."

"A prince and a champion, eh ?" exclaimed the Emperor. "And you would be a soldier and fight for your emperor, even as your father fought for his king ? Well, perhaps if we could but have you washed, we might find something worth the training, under the dirt. It is on the old Tower wharf they are to meet the man from England. Was that what you said ?"

"Yes, Sire,— this very night—at the stroke of nine — near to where the old gate used to stand," the boy prompted, as the Emperor noted the time upon the memorandum he had made; while little Prince Napoleon, tired of all this talk, tugged at the long gray overcoat, and renewed his demand: "A ride on sheep. Baby wants to ride again, Uncle Bibiche."

But the antelopes, despairing of any further gifts of snuff, had long since trotted off, and "Uncle Bibiche" was occupied with thoughts of other matters.

His whistle-call sounded again, and once more the foresters appeared.

"Take this boy to Monsieur Corson, clerk of the kitchen; bid him give the little man a dinner and a gold napoleon; afterward, see that he is returned to the city in a cab. And mind, you boy — not a word of what you have told me to Mother Thérèse, nor to Babette."

"Not even to Babette, Sire," the boy replied.

"For the rest, I will make proof of your hearing, and, should your ears have done me service, they shall hear yet better things. Uncle Bibiche never forgets; does he, Monseigneur Little One ?"

But the baby Prince replied, as the Emperor caught him up, "Uncle Bibiche forgets Baby's ride."

"So! Does he? Then shall he ride pickaback." And, swinging the child up to the imperial shoulders, the Emperor of France galloped off up the avenue with the son of the King of Holland. Then the boy from Paris followed the foresters to the clerk of the kitchen, and in the scullion's quarters had an excellent dinner, received a golden napoleon, and rode back like a prince to the narrow and dirty Street of the Washerwomen, in the slums of Paris.

Here, however, trouble awaited him. The cab and the golden napoleon secured for him momentary glory, though his story that he had seen and talked with the Little Corporal was openly scoffed at by all save Babette.

Mother Thérèse confiscated the napoleon, and regarded the cab as but the ending of only another of "that boy's scrapes," and prophesied, as indeed she generally did once a day, that he would come to no good end, for all her bringing up. But the boy held stoutly to his promise, and claimed only to have been to St. Cloud and to have talked with the Emperor. It must be admitted that he made the most of this; and, while his glittering story of princes and palaces found an absorbed and loyal listener in little Babette, the boys of the quarter made sport of it all as "one of the mud prince's fairy tales." They even went so far as to say that Philip had snatched the golden napoleon from some sight-seeing countryman on the Boulevard, and that the police would be after him for it; while as for the cab-ride, they declared that was in return for some job done for a driver who had more room in his cab than money in his pocket.

That "pig of a Pierre over the way" stoutly asserted, indeed, that the mud prince was "in" with some of the light-fingered gentry of the Court of the Miracles near by,—the thieves' quarter of old Paris,—and would get "come up with" yet. This was the burden of Pierre's taunting song all that afternoon. It was renewed next morning, until "the prince" could stand it no longer, and a battle royal ensued by the little stone-coped fountain at the head of the Street of the Washerwomen.

All the street gathered to witness the battle, and opinion differed as to its possible issue, for now Pierre and now "the prince" was down.

But, just as Pierre had been thrown for the last time, and was about to admit his defeat, two gendarmes, or armed policemen, thrust their way through the crowd and "nabbed" the victor.

"You boy, you live with Mother Thérèse, do you not?" one of the policemen inquired.

"To be sure I do," the boy replied, looking defiantly on his questioner—held to be a foe by every street-boy, as all policemen are.

"You are Philip, son of the émigré Desnouettes, bound out to the citizeness Thérèse Rapin, laundress, of the Street of the Washerwomen?"

"As all the quarter knows, and you as well," Philip admitted without hesitation.

The policeman turned to a grim man in plain clothes who stood close at hand. "This is our boy, Monsieur the Prefect. I thought I knew him."

"Bring him along, then," the prefect commanded.

"'COME, YOU BOY; YOU ARE TO GO WITH US,' THE POLICEMAN SAID."

"Come, you boy; you are to go with us," the policeman said.

"But where—and why?" Philip asked.

"That you will know later," answered the officer. "Come." And with his hand on Philip's shoulder, he led the boy away, following the prefect and the other gendarme.

Then, while one of the boys, proud to be the bearer of evil tidings, rushed down the Street of the Washerwomen to notify Mother Thérèse of what had happened, and while Babette, seeing her only champion dragged away to prison, lifted up her voice in a long, loud wail of fear and sorrow, that "pig of a Pierre," rising from the scene of his defeat, danced the mad dance of joy and triumph, and, shaking his grimy fist at the retreating Philip, shouted after him:

"Yah, mud prince, pickpocket! Yah, I told you so!"

And it must be confessed that most of the quarter saw in this only the sequel to the golden napoleon and the "Emperor's cab" story, and echoed Pierre's unfriendly "I told you so!"

But Philip, marveling inwardly at his sudden and unlooked-for taking off, went with his captors without word or question. "The time for talk is when the time arrives," he reasoned shrewdly.

And so, speechless, he was marched away—he knew not where nor why.

CHAPTER III

THE SCHOOL-BOY OF ST. CYR

HE found out speedily. As they passed from the Street of the Washerwomen into the Street of the Night Patrol, and so on beside the ruins of the great castle, Philip thought they were taking him to the office of the chief of police in the splendid City Hall; but, passing the Square of the River Beach, upon which faced the statued front of the City Hall, the boy's conductors pushed ahead without stopping, cut across into the long Street of the Temple, and as before them loomed the four gray turrets and the great central tower, Philip knew his destination to be the gloomy old Temple itself—the death-chamber of knights and kings.

"Come, now, this is pleasant!" he said to himself, wondering why they should take him there. "What am I, then? He who picks a pocket or steals a ride is surely too small game for the Temple. It is there they take traitors and assassins. And, surely, I am neither."

So, wondering still, he passed through the frowning gateway of the Temple, and speedily stood within one of the "examination chambers," in which were gathered certain men, some in uniform and some in citizen's dress.

Then, indeed, did Philip give a start of surprise, and fathom the reason for his forced march; for among those gathered in the examination chamber he recognized at once "the three rascally ones" whom, in the wine-shop of Citizen Popon, he had heard conspiring against the Emperor.

The boy was confronted with the men, and swore to their identity without hesitation. He could never have forgotten them. His testimony was almost unnecessary; for, so cleverly had they, with "the man from England," been entrapped upon the wharf of the Tower, that the police had a clear case against them from the start. But Philip's evidence was the connecting link, and the would-be assassins of the Emperor came to speedy punishment. They simply "disappeared," so the record says: but that means a swift and secret punishment. And that is all we hear of the conspiracy of Louis Loizeau, "the man from England," whose plotting this boy of ten so cleverly brought to naught.

His evidence thus given, the boy of ten came quickly into his reward. Under the guidance of an officer from the central police, he visited the shops in the straggling arcades of the old Temple market, and came out a new boy — clean, clothed, and almost a stranger to himself, fit to call on the king.

Such a call was, evidently, next on the program; for soon a cab was whirling him, with many a twist and turn, through broad boulevard and narrow street, and so across the Seine into the open country and the smiling park of St. Cloud.

This time he did not loiter under the great chestnut-trees, nor was he handed over to the clerk of the kitchen, nor left in the "scullion's quarters." Straight to the noble palace he was driven, and then, under the guidance of Constant, the Emperor's body-servant, he was led to the private apartments in the great palace of St. Cloud. And there, once more, he saw the Emperor.

Before a closed door the valet stopped and rapped. Then he flung it open and announced: "The boy from Paris, Sire."

Not in royal robes, nor yet in the glittering uniform of the chief soldier of France, did the boy from Paris find the Emperor. He simply saw "Uncle Bibiche" once more! For there, pacing up and down the room, head bent and hands clasped behind his back, as if in thought, walked the short, stout man in a simple uniform. And strutting after him, almost on his heels, came the little four-year-old antelope-rider, with the Emperor's famous little chapeau covering his curly head, and the Emperor's terrible "sword of Marengo" trailing on the floor behind him.

The "boy from Paris" entered the room. The Emperor looked up and, with a smile of surprise at the boy's altered appearance, exclaimed: "But not our dirty boy, little one! Our prince of the sans-culottes looks as fine as a fiddler, does he not? How is it, son of the *émigré*? Is the mud prince on the road to being a gold prince?"

Even Philip's uncomfortableness in his new clothes—an uncomfortableness that was almost an imprisonment after the liberty of rags, for it made him feel, as he expressed it, "all hands and feet"—could not keep back the laugh that sprang from his quick sense of the ridiculous, at sight of Uncle Bibiche and the little caricature at his heels, bearing the famous hat and sword. But he collected himself speedily, and replied to the imperial "funning."

"I am come, Sire," he said, "because they sent me here. I thank you for my fine clothes."

"THE EMPEROR'S FAMOUS CHAPEAU COVERING HIS CURLY HEAD, AND THE EMPEROR'S 'SWORD OF MARENGO' TRAILING ON THE FLOOR BEHIND HIM."

"As I thank you for your open ears, mud prince," responded the Emperor, giving to the boy's ear the pinch that was always the sign of Napoleon's good humor. "They may have saved my life, these ears; though you will live to learn that it is one thing to plot and another to do. And what now—would you still wish to go for a soldier?"

"If the Emperor will," the boy replied.

"So; that is what you told Babette. And how is Babette?" the Emperor asked.

"Weeping sorely, Sire, because the policeman carried me off, just when I had knocked down that pig of a Pierre for calling me a pickpocket."

"Ah, then you left the Street of the Washerwomen in disgrace, you boy? So! Then shall you go back there in glory. But not to stay there. Son of the *émigré* Desnouettes, I will make you a soldier of France."

Overjoyed at this sudden coming true of his fondest dream, Philip fairly flung himself at the feet of the Emperor in a transport of joy, whereupon little Prince Napoleon, thinking the boy from Paris was there for his pleasure, danced about and said:

"Sing 'Zig-zag' again, Dirty Boy. Sing 'Zig-zag' again."

Philip struggled to his feet. "Shall I, Sire?" and Napoleon nodded assent.

Then around and around the room the boy and the baby capered, for thus could Philip best work off his excess of rapture. And, as they capered, they sang again the chorus:

"Zig-zag; rig-a-doon,
 Dance away to the drumstick's tune!"

Suddenly Philip stopped.

"And Babette, Sire?" he inquired.

"Well—what of Babette?" said the Emperor. "She may not go as a soldier."

"No, Sire. But I can look after her no more if I march away, and Mother Thérèse is a wicked one. And the Street of the Washerwomen is not for such as Babette. And the Emperor can do all things."

"Not all things. But this he can do. He can send you to school, and then make you a soldier. He can send Babette to school, and then make her a lady — or one fit to be a lady. She must not disgrace the prince, her champion. She, too, shall go to school."

Again Philip could not restrain himself; and, in excess of joy, hugged his friend the little Prince, who still clung to his hand.

"And—am I to go now, Sire?" he asked, after a moment.

"It is never too early to begin the making of a soldier of France," the Emperor said. Then he clapped his hands, and Constant entered quickly.

"Constant," the Emperor said, "find Monsieur Meneval. Bid him meet me in my cabinet."

Then the Emperor left the two boys alone, and Philip told the little Prince stories of Babette and the boys of the washerwomen's quarter, while the little Prince recited for Philip one of La Fontaine's fables, many of which the bright little fellow knew by heart.

But before he had gone through "King Log," Constant appeared again, and Philip was taken to the Emperor. With him was an officer of the household.

"Go with Monsieur my secretary, young Desnouettes. He will conduct you to the Street of the Washerwomen, and change disgrace to honor. He will see to Babette. He will place you in the military school of Fontainebleau, now transferred to St. Cyr. There shall you learn a soldier's first duty—obedience; a soldier's single watchward—loyalty. Be studious, be attentive, be obedient, be loyal, be honorable, son of the *émigré* Desnouettes, and your future may be a brilliant one. I shall hear of you. Farewell."

He motioned the lad out; but ere the boy turned to go, he stammered out words full of joy and thankfulness. "Sire," he said, "you shall hear of me. I will be true, and—thank you for Babette."

Then he followed Monsieur the Secretary, and was soon speeding away with him in one of the household carriages, on the panel of which was emblazoned the imperial "N."

Straight to the dirty Street of the Washerwomen the carriage sped. And what a time there was in that dark and narrow quarter of the old city when the carriage drew up before the little coped fountain where "that pig of a Pierre" had shaken the fist of derision and contempt!

And when from the carriage stepped the boy in his new suit, with Monsieur the Emperor's secretary, and Monsieur the deputy mayor of the section (the alderman of the ward, as one might say), following after, then how the people stared!

And when Monsieur the deputy mayor in a loud voice announced that for gallant action and for loyal deed his imperial majesty the Emperor took into his service Philip, the son of the *émigré* Desnouettes, how the people cheered!

Then Mother Thérèse, that foxy old tyrant, "blessed the boy," and did not see how she could spare him, and took the purse of money the Emperor sent her, while "that pig of a Pierre over the way" turned so green with envy that Philip really felt sorry for him.

And how little Babette laughed and cried in the same breath when Philip told her the Emperor had heard about her and meant to make a lady of her!

So it was soon over, for all the world like some wonderful fairy tale, and Philip Desnouettes, son of the *émigré*, bound boy of the washerwomen's quarter, protégé of the Emperor, turned his back upon the narrow and dirty street he had once called his home, and, riding away from the past, was entered as a pupil in the military school of St. Cyr.

From the day when, as a new boy, he was introduced into the new school of St. Cyr, and was gradually transformed from an uncouth street-boy to a little machine, to the day when, four years later, he left it for other scenes, Philip Desnouettes's life was one of continuous training. He got up by the drum, he ate his meals by the drum, he went to bed by the drum. He learned to drill, to ride, and to build fortifications; he received instruction in languages, literature, history, and mathematics; he toughened without fires, developed by austere discipline, lived by rule, played pranks and took his punishment as he did his medicine—without grumbling; he grew, strengthened, broadened in mind and body, learned to be a French school-boy, a French soldier, a French gentleman.

Then came 1810. Great things had been happening while Philip was a school-boy at St. Cyr. The map of Europe

CADET DESNOUETTES AND CORPORAL PEYROLLES.—"'BE A SOLDIER OF FRANCE!'"

had been changed again and again, and Napoleon was the map-maker. There had been wars and rumors of war; there had been mighty marches, bloody battles, terrible triumphs; and with march and battle and triumph the fame of Napoleon, Emperor of the French, had grown to mighty proportions. In 1810 France and Napoleon were the greatest names in all the world. And Philip had met Corporal Peyrolles.

Peyrolles, the wooden-legged, had left his good leg of flesh on the bloody field of Austerlitz, and, pensioned by the Emperor, had been made one of the drill-sergeants in St. Cyr school.

To Peyrolles the Emperor was not a man, he was "the Emperor"; and Peyrolles worshiped him even as did the Romans of old worship their highest and bravest—as something more than mortal. And yet the boys of St. Cyr declared that but for Peyrolles the Emperor would never have been; for it was Peyrolles's delight to recount for the boys of St. Cyr how "I and the Emperor" conquered the world!

But it was largely by Peyrolles's friendly promptings, *plus* the instruction of the St. Cyr school, that Philip became proficient in drill and ambitious of glory. And when, even before the allotted term of training, the summons came to "the cadet Desnouettes" to attend upon the Emperor, the boy felt that both fame and glory lay well within his grasp.

But Peyrolles said, "See what it is to have Corporal Peyrolles for your friend, cadet. Do you think it is because your sharp ears served the Emperor, when you were but a boy of the streets, that he now calls you to his side, even before your military schooling is done? Not so. It is because of me. It is because Peyrolles has had you in hand. The Emperor has heard of it. He bids you come to him that you may show others in his service what it is to be tutored in arms by the man who helped the Emperor to win the day at Arcola and Lodi, at Castiglione and the Pyramids, at Marengo and Ulm and Austerlitz. Long live the Emperor, and long live Peyrolles, his right hand! Do not disgrace my teaching. You are but an infant yet, cadet. But so were we all once, and even a child can be brave. Listen, you cadet: rush not rashly into danger, but, once in, do not back out. Strike not until you can strike swift and sure. Obey, and you shall be obeyed; follow, and you shall be followed; seek glory, and glory shall seek you. Be a soldier of France, and France shall be proud of her soldier, and shall say to the world: 'Behold, this cadet was a pupil of Peyrolles of St. Cyr, grenadier and helper of the Emperor!'"

So Philip left St. Cyr and reported at the Tuileries, that noble old palace in the city, whose story is interwoven with that of France's ups and downs through fully three hundred years.

And in Napoleon's private study, beyond the Diana Gallery and next to the Blue Room, Philip once more saluted the Emperor.

"So, it is young Desnouettes, the boy with the good ears," was the Emperor's greeting. "Have both eyes and ears served you well at St. Cyr, you cadet? You look a little soldier already. Are you prepared to march and to fight?"

"Yes, Sire — for the Emperor," the boy replied shrewdly.

"Good"; and Napoleon pulled the cadet's hair good-humoredly. "But these are no longer days of blood. The empire is at peace. I have sent for you to serve here at court. Take your orders from the Baron de Meneval. From this day you are a page of the palace."

CHAPTER IV

THE BALL AT THE EMBASSY

IT was a new life into which this imperial appointment plunged the active boy of fourteen. It was discipline, and yet it was delightful; it was slavery, and yet it was splendor; there was labor to tire both feet and brain; there were long hours of monotony, but many opportunities for pranks and frolics. It was run here and run there; it was do this and do that; it was not soldiering, and yet it had its conflicts; it was not a call for courage, and yet it was duty joined to temptation and tried by opportunity. The life of a page of the palace was not all play, though passed in the midst of splendor; nor was it all dignity, though spent in a constant round of fête and ceremonial.

And into fête and ceremonial young Philip Desnouettes was speedily introduced. It was the year 1810. In that year Napoleon the Emperor married the Archduchess of Austria. The son of a poor Corsican office-seeker wedded the daughter of the Austrian Cæsars. It was a year of brilliancy, of excitement, of restless rounds of display and constant repetitions of marvelous entertainments.

Never was a boy of fourteen surrounded by more of glitter, or permitted to be a part of more royal "goings on." All this might ruin a boy of weak nature; but Philip was blessed with a cool head, a well-balanced mind, and much common sense. He had "cut his wisdom-teeth" as a street-boy of Paris; he had learned discipline in the school of St. Cyr; and so, though often sorely tried and many a time in scrapes and in disgrace, he was too manly a fellow to "lose his head." He was therefore really developed alike by the temptations and by the duties that filled his daily life in those most brilliant surroundings—the court of the First Empire.

As page of the palace, he was on duty both at the splendid Tuileries and at beautiful St. Cloud. And through the month of March there was enough afoot in both these great palaces to tire any ordinary boy, and keep his head buzzing with bewilderment. For then it was that Paris and the palaces were making ready for the reception of the new mistress of France, the girl Empress, Marie Louise, Archduchess of Austria.

Philip could not understand it all. Austria had been "a red rag" to every French boy since the days of Marie Antoinette. And at St. Cyr Philip had been brought up to hate the Austrians, with whom the Emperor was so often at war, and whom, three times, he had faced and conquered.

"I would like to know what Peyrolles thinks of this," he often said to himself. "The Emperor marry an Austrian? Well, for one, I can't see through it!"

But what of that? No boy of fourteen gives much thought to political right or wrong, or wastes time over the policy of kings and cabinets. Only the events that bring him opportunity, or the doings that mean excitement and fun, arouse in him anticipation and desire.

He ran here and he ran there; he fetched and he carried;

he rehearsed for ceremonies and waited for orders at palace doors; he "bossed things" whenever he had a little brief authority; he did the thousand and one "chores" that are a part of the duties of a royal page, who is above servants in station and below officials in rank. The Grand Marshal of the Palace, the Chief Secretary to the Emperor, the First Gentleman in Waiting, the First Page of the Palace, and, first of all, the Emperor himself—these were the boy's masters. As became a royal page, he ignored all others, and gave himself airs whenever he was beyond the beck and call of his acknowledged superiors.

Fête crowned fête, and ceremony ceremony. By stately stages, from Vienna on to Paris, the Austrian princess came to her throne, escorted by peers of France, and surrounded by all the pomp and power of this theatrical First Empire. Then Napoleon met her; and on a bright April day she entered Paris in a blaze of glory.

And Philip entered, too, so spick and span in a new and gorgeous livery that he felt certain all eyes must be looking at him quite as much as at any one who had a place in that long and glittering procession escorting Napoleon and Louise from St. Cloud to the Tuileries.

And where do you think the boy was? Clinging with five other pages, for all the world as if they were "cutting behind," to the foot-board of the magnificent coronation coach of glass and gold in which sat the Emperor and Empress. For there, according to the etiquette that governed the imperial "show," was the place for the pages, while as many more hung on to the driver's seat; and I really believe the boys and girls of Paris thought it almost as fine to be one of those clinging pages as to be the Emperor in his cloak of red and white velvet, or the Empress by his side, glittering in her golden dress and her circlet of diamonds. I am sure Babette thought so, when she spied Philip. For Babette was one of the throng of little girls, dressed in white, who at the Arch of Triumph showered the coronation coach with flowers, and sang a welcome to the new Empress.

So, under great arches and along the crowded streets, which were gorgeously decorated and lined with tiers of seats built for the people, with the imperial cavalry in advance, with lancers and chasseurs and dragoons marching in splendid array, with bands playing their best, with heralds-at-arms in brilliant costumes, and with eight prancing horses drawing the coronation coach topped with its golden dome, its four spread eagles, and its imperial crown, Philip and the Emperor brought the girl Empress into Paris.

The bells rang merrily, the artillery thundered salutes, the picked soldiers of the Grand Army in double files along the route presented arms, the young girls strewed the way with flowers, the great marshals of France and the colonels of the Imperial Guard, mounted on their splendid horses, surrounded the glittering coach. Thus, up the shouting Champs Elysées,—real " Fields of Paradise " that day,—and under the great arch into the Tuileries gardens, this splendid procession moved to where, in the magnificent Square Room of the palace of the Tuileries, Napoleon and Louise, surrounded by kings and queens, by lords and ladies, by cardinals and priests, and in the presence of eight thousand invited guests, were married by the Cardinal Fesch, Grand Almoner of France and uncle of the Emperor.

It was a regal display, one of the few really gorgeous ceremonials of history. Not the least interested spectator was young Philip Desnouettes, as, with the throng of royal pages, he crowded upon the steps that led to the great platform on which the marriage ceremony took place. Then followed the promenade in the picture-gallery, the reception in the splendid Hall of the Marshals, the imperial banquet in the theater, the public concert in the vast amphitheater built in the Tuileries gardens, the fireworks all along the Champs Elysées, the illumination of the Tuileries and of the great avenues and bridges and buildings of the city, which blazed with light until, as Philip declared, "all Paris seemed on fire."

He missed a part of the show, however, because he had a special duty to perform. He had to keep a dog from barking.

Into a room of the Tuileries he had been introduced by young Master Malvirade, the very important First Page to the Emperor, and had been ordered to wait there until relieved.

"There's a dog in here," the First Page had told him, "and a parrot. See to it, young Desnouettes, that the dog does not bark, nor the parrot squawk."

Here was a nice job for a boy who wished to see the fireworks! Philip was almost tempted to rebel; but he had been trained to obey, and he said not a word.

The room was at the end of a long corridor that was narrow and dimly lighted, but in the room itself there was a blaze of light from many lamps and candles. Philip had never seen this room before, and looked at it critically. It was clearly not a state apartment; it was more homelike than handsome. There were drawings and paintings on the walls, the furniture was not new, and certainly not Paris-made. Here hung some tapestry-work; there, birds in cages. On a gilded perch a great green parrot was clawing and shifting, cocking one bright eye down at a little dog crouched on a rug below him. It was this dog and this parrot that Philip was to keep quiet.

He waited some time. The cheers of the crowd in the garden and the sounds of the great chorus at the open-air concert came, muffled, to his ears. The parrot was uneasy; the dog was restless; so, too, was Philip, and he grumbled inwardly at his imprisonment; but, all the same, he did his duty, petted the dog, and soothed "poor Polly" with promises of make-believe crackers.

At last he heard steps coming along the corridor. The parrot cocked its head to listen; the dog started up and tried to "woof," but Philip's hand smothered the incipient bark.

The door opened, and a lady entered. She was young,— scarcely more than a girl,—but she was splendidly dressed, and her face was pretty and pleasant.

She stopped, blinded at first by the flood of light after the dimness of the corridor. Then she looked about her, started suddenly, and as the dog, with a bark and a struggle, broke away from Philip and sprang toward her, she dropped on her knees, regardless of her splendid dress, and fondled the dog with a cry of joy.

"Why, it is my room!" she cried, looking about in bewilderment,—"my own room at Vienna! The very same carpet, the very same chairs, my sister Clementine's drawings, my mother's tapestry, my uncle Charles's paintings, my books, my birds—Polly—and you—you dear, dear Fritz-kin!" here she hugged the little dog again. Then she sprang to her feet, and, saying impulsively, "Oh, Sire, how kind you are!" flung her arms about the neck of the gentleman who had followed her into the room,—a short, stout middle-aged gentleman, with a splendid court costume, and a handsome face that sparkled with pleasure at the success of his little plot. It was Napoleon, and this was his surprise to his girl wife. He had reproduced in the Tuileries the room she had tearfully said good-by to in her father's palace at Vienna; he had remembered everything—even to the dog and the parrot that were her especial pets.

It was such a successful surprise that fun-loving Philip could not keep back the smile of sympathy.

"So, it is you, young Desnouettes; you are the genie in charge, eh?" the Emperor said. "Louise, this page once saved my life from plotters; and now, behold! he is in a plot against the Empress. There's gratitude for you!"

The girl Empress cast a bright, quick look of pleasure at the kneeling boy, and held out to him a hand which Philip loyally kissed, swearing fealty to her in his chivalrous young heart. And the Empress never forgot him, amid all the strange faces and crowding scenes of her new life as a sovereign.

Through the spring and into the summer these faces and scenes thronged, one upon the other, in quick succession. In April the Emperor and Empress, on their wedding journey, made "a progress" through northern France; during May and June festivity followed festivity in Paris, so closely and with such grandeur that Philip really grew weary of

"THE EMPRESS HELD OUT A HAND WHICH PHILIP LOYALLY KISSED."

magnificence. Finally, on the first day of July, came the conclusion of this series of grand entertainments in honor of the Emperor and Empress—the ball at the Austrian Embassy.

In his fine old mansion on the Street of Provence, sometimes known as Hospital Road, and sometimes known as the Street of the Crooked Stocking, the Austrian ambassador, Prince Schwarzenberg, gave a great ball. The house was not large enough for the entertainment he wished to give, so in his garden he built, "for one night only," a great wooden ball-room.

It was so splendidly decorated and furnished that it looked like a fairy palace. Its walls were covered with gold and silver brocade; draperies of spangled gauze were festooned all about it, fastened with flowers and glittering ornaments; while lights from chandeliers and candelabra made the great ball-room as brilliant as day.

The guests entered this splendid "palace for a night" through a long gallery that connected it with the mansion. Musicians played in the Court of Honor; grottoes and arbors and temples were scattered all about the garden; on the lawn brilliantly costumed dancers took part in a delightful spectacle, and in the ball-room itself nearly two thousand people began to dance at midnight.

Philip was there, too — semi-officially on duty as a royal page, but also in for a good time as a guest of the ambassador.

He was having such a good time! There were plenty of young people there; and though, of course, the pages could hardly be expected to dance in the great ball-room, the boys found partners somehow, as boys are wont to do when such a fine chance for a dance occurs. To the same music that guided the grand quadrille in the ball-room, the boys and girls started an impromptu quadrille on the lawn, and had, no doubt, a much better time than the great folks at the stately function inside.

Philip found himself dancing with a pretty girl of about his own age, whose name he failed to catch in the hurried introduction that made her his partner; but they enjoyed their dance quite as much as if they had always known each other. And when the first quadrille was over, the boys and girls crowded into the big ball-room to see the Emperor make his progress through the room, and to watch the young Empress as, throned on the imperial platform, she talked with two queens and a king or two.

In the Court of Honor the trumpets sounded a flourish; in the Temple of Glory a song of triumph was being sung; everything was brightness and beauty and gaiety and brilliancy, when, suddenly, Philip saw several gentlemen dash into the throng; then he heard a shout of warning, a note of terror; there came another rush, and above the flourish of the trumpets and the voices of the singers rang out the cry:

"Fire, fire!—the ball-room is on fire!"

It was no false alarm. The draperies caught quickly; the hangings burst into a blaze; there was a mad race for the one doorway that led into the house, and everywhere were confusion, terror, and a desperate dash for life.

Philip caught by the arm the young girl with whom he had been dancing on the lawn.

"Quick, give me your hand, mademoiselle!" he cried; "trust me, and I will save you. The garden is our best chance."

But the girl seemed dazed. "My father!—where is my father?" she cried. "Oh, find my father!"

Philip was as wiry as he was plucky and sturdy, but an excited crowd in a blazing ball-room knows neither courage nor courtesy where all are struggling to escape.

Even as he lost his hold of the girl's arm when she sought to dart off in another direction, the splendidly dressed mob surged in between, and, separating the two, flung the boy to the floor, where he lay, trampled upon and kicked about in this mad rush for safety.

And, as he fell, he heard above the uproar the terrible danger-call: "A plot, a plot! Frenchmen, defend your Emperor!"

CHAPTER V

IN THE STREET OF THE FIGHT

TWISTING and squirming with a persistency that would do credit to a modern foot-ball scrimmage, Philip wriggled his way from beneath those trampling feet, and at last stood erect—battered, but whole.

He looked about him for an instant, striving to catch his breath and get his bearings. It was a scene of terror and despair. The great room was thick with smoke, the flames were already roaring up to the roof, and seemed to burst from the house with which the ball-room was connected. Cries and shrieks filled the air. There is nothing more terrible than a mob gone mad with fright and fear. In this one were displayed those tragic and ludicrous phases of excitable human nature, which so often loses its head in great crises, and does so many ridiculous things.

Some, however, kept their wits about them, and worked like Trojans. By dint of much labor they cleared the blocked doorway, and hurried the throng into the garden and the street beyond. About the Emperor, Philip saw a ring of the officers of the Imperial Guard, who with drawn swords kept the surging mob at bay, while he heard above the turmoil the voice of the Austrian ambassador shouting to Napoleon, "My life for yours, Sire! If this is a plot, it shall strike me dead before it touches you!"

And on the imperial platform, calmly seated on the throne, Philip, with a flush of pride in her courage, saw the girl Empress, the coolest one in all that excited crowd, quietly awaiting the word of her husband, the Emperor, to leave the place with him.

There was no plot. The fire was but a fearful accident that was to wreck the beautiful building and bring death to many homes. Assured of this, Napoleon worked his way to the platform, took the Empress by the hand, hurried into the garden, and, placing her in a carriage which Philip had found for him, sent his wife in safety to St. Cloud. Then he returned to the scene of disaster, and, in the same spirit of command that made so many of his battles victories, worked amid ruin and smoke to save life and property.

Philip worked too. As excited and omnipresent, and probably quite as much in the way, as a boy always is at a big fire, he rushed hither and thither, helping and hindering alike, but anxious above all things to find the pretty little partner who had been swept from his side when the rush had overthrown and trampled him under foot.

He feared the worst. How could any girl escape what a boy had been unable to withstand? Burning beams were falling; now an overcrowded staircase gave way and collapsed; now the great chandelier came crashing down; the lost were crying; the wounded were calling for help, and a sudden storm bursting upon the doomed building fanned the flames into a roaring blaze.

Rushing along one of the garden walks, determined to

search everywhere for the missing girl, Philip stumbled into a half-concealed grotto in which a band of musicians had been stationed for an outdoor concert. There, in the wreckage of overturned music-racks and forsaken instruments, Philip saw the body of a young girl. It was she whom he sought. Overcome by the smoke, or by the fright and frenzy of the stampede, she had evidently found a place of refuge and then comfortably fainted.

Of course Philip thought she was dead. "Oh, Mademoiselle!" he cried in despair.

But even as he raised her up, she recovered consciousness, looked about her dazed, and then called, "Father!—Oh, take me to my father!"

Philip recalled the stories of Bayard and Roland, and all the gallant knights of old who had succored maidens in distress. Here, now, was his chance to show himself a true chevalier.

"Mademoiselle, let me take you home," he said. "Your father is there, no doubt."

Still weak from her fall and fright, the girl leaned upon her protector, and they made their way through the garden to the street. A tardy fire-engine, as clumsy as it was useless, rolled lumbering up to the gateway, and Philip drew the girl aside to avoid a collision with the excited crowd that came with it.

Suddenly the girl gave a cry of joy.

"Father, father!" she called shrilly; and, breaking from her conductor's side, she sprang into the arms of a gentleman whose look of mingled misery and perplexity changed swiftly into one of relief and joy as he clasped the girl in a welcome that was also protection. Then they turned, and before Philip could reach them they had hurried through the gateway, and were lost in the crowd and the darkness.

"Well," said Philip, just a trifle chagrined at this unexpected ending to his attempt at knight-errantry, "she is safe, no doubt. If one might have known her name! I wonder who she is?"

Then, finding that some order was coming out of the chaos of disaster, and that the firemen, the soldiers, and the armed police had taken matters in charge, Philip concluded there was no more to be seen. Wet and smoky, disheveled and torn, he started for the Tuileries; but as he crossed the square near the Vendôme Column he spied a carriage with pages on the box pushing its way through the crowd.

"Holo you! To St. Cloud?" he shouted in inquiry. And a chorus of pages replied:

"To St. Cloud, yes! Where have you tumbled from, disreputable one? Come along, my Lord Mud and Soot! Climb up here, young Desnouettes." Philip clambered up without even stopping the coach, and, squeezing himself in among the pages, was soon chattering and clattering away to St. Cloud and a brief night's rest.

Early next morning, by order of the Emperor, he hurried to the Embassy for the latest news. He brought back sorry tidings. The destruction of the mansion was complete. Many had been injured; some had been killed outright, or had since died. Altogether it was a tragic ending to what had promised to be a brilliant affair.

But those were days when people were all too familiar with disaster and death. Crowding events pushed past happenings out of mind. Napoleon wished his court to be both gay and glorious, and disaster must never be mentioned.

So the fatal ball at the Embassy was forgotten, save by those who had experienced its terrors, either to their own hurt or in the injury or loss of those who were dear to them. The coming of new glories gave a fresh current to thought, while new happenings occupied young and old, rich and poor, in Paris.

Once a week, when off duty for a few hours, Philip always went to see Babette. He took as much interest in her education and progress as if he were indeed her guardian, and the sisters of the convent school in the Street of the Old Pigeon-House (or, as they called it in Paris, the Rue du Vieux-Colombier) welcomed the bright boy with smiles, and allowed him a generous half-hour's interview in the conversation room.

There was enough of the street-boy nature remaining in Philip to make him like to "prowl"; and in these walks to see Babette in the Street of the Old Pigeon-House, the young page of the palace would, therefore, often make roundabout journeys. He stumbled into all sorts of out-of-the-way places, ran all sorts of risks, but never fell into any real danger, though there was plenty of it beneath the surface life in the Paris of those days.

It was while on one of his "prowls," one afternoon, when he had been to visit Babette, that he was strolling leisurely along the Street of the Fight (known to Parisians as the Rue de Mêlée), one of the very quietest and quaintest of the streets of the old city, when he was attracted by a tug of war between two hostile sparrows which were struggling for a tough straw that both seemed equally to fancy for nest-repairing.

The sparrows pulled and tugged and fluttered so vigorously that Philip, always alive to the humorous side of things, leaned against the nearest fence-rail and watched the equal match.

"Perhaps that's why they call this the Fight Street," he was just saying to himself, when he felt a touch on his shoulder. Looking up, he saw a decent-looking house-servant.

"Will Monsieur enter?" the man said. "Mademoiselle receives."

Philip looked puzzled. "Mademoiselle?" he queried.

"Yes, Monsieur," the footman explained; "the Citizen Keeper's daughter. She saw you from the window, and her father, the Keeper, sends me to bid you enter. To-day Mademoiselle receives."

Philip looked closely at the house. He was certain he had never seen it before.

"But," he began, "I do not know Mademoiselle."

At that instant a tall, scholarly-looking gentleman came through the open doorway and stood beside him.

"Oh, but you do, my boy," he said, breaking in upon Philip's uncertainty. "Enter, I beg, and see for yourself."

The gentleman was so distinguished in appearance, and he laid so friendly a hand upon the page's shoulder, that Philip flung hesitation to the winds and willingly entered the house.

The footman lifted a heavy curtain, and Philip stood within a neat drawing-room furnished in the simple style of the Revolution. A young girl came quickly forward from a group of people.

"I am so glad you came in," she said impulsively. "I saw you from the window, and knew you at once."

Philip looked closely at the speaker. In an instant it was all clear to him. "Mademoiselle" was his partner in the quadrille on the lawn—the girl he had rescued from the grotto that fatal night of the ball at the Embassy.

He bent low over her extended hand, for thus were boys of those days taught to "make their manners" to ladies.

"Mademoiselle is very kind," he said.

The girl laughed merrily at this stately politeness, and, making up for the forgotten ceremony with which she should have greeted him after the fashion of the day, she courtesied deeply in acknowledgment. Then she laughed again joyfully and unaffectedly.

"Did you not think us most ungrateful, we two—my father and I," she said, "that we should have so rushed away from you that dreadful night? But my father—why, where is he? See, my father, was I not right?—it was our benefactor."

Philip's conductor gave him a cordial smile of welcome. He took both the lad's hands in his. "My best of boys," he cried, "how proud I am to see you here! We have long wished—we two thoughtless ones—to learn who was the brave young gentleman who united us that dreadful night—"

"When we lost our schottische," interrupted Mademoiselle. "Do you not remember that was next to come when the wreaths caught fire?"

"And such a charming schottische as it would have been," said Philip gallantly.

"Let me make you known to our friends," said the master of the house, as he took the boy's arm and hurried him toward the waiting group. "My friends," he said, "let me present to you —"

Here his daughter again interrupted him. "But, papa," she cried, "we do not know Monsieur's name — nor does he know ours. Is it not droll?"

"So! the little one is right," said the introducer, with a laugh. "Permit me, Monsieur. We are the household of Daunou, Keeper of the Archives. I am the Keeper. Mademoiselle here is my dear daughter Lucie. And you?"

"I, Monsieur the Keeper," replied the boy, "am Philip Desnouettes, one of the pages to the Emperor."

"Ha, that Corsican!" The exclamation came from a little fat man of middle age and fierce face, who stood at the elbow of Monsieur the Keeper of the Archives.

Philip fired up in an instant.

"Sir, I said the Emperor!" he exclaimed, a flush of surprise and anger mantling his face.

"Pouf, pouf! What a young game-cock it is! How hot we are! And is he not a Corsican?" the fat man fumed.

But the Keeper of the Archives clapped a hand over the offending mouth. "Be quiet, Fauriel," he said. "Monsieur the Page is my guest, and such words are not for him. We all have our preferences and our loyalties. Desnouettes, did you say, my boy?"

"Yes, Monsieur; Philip Desnouettes," the boy replied.

"The name has a familiar sound," said the Keeper. "Your father?"

"An *émigré*, Monsieur," the boy answered. "Executed in 1796 for not leaving France when the nobles were that year expelled."

"What, you boy!" Fauriel the fat broke in; "your father a martyr, and you a slave of the Corsican!"

"Sir, my Emperor was not the murderer of my father; he has been my protector," Philip began, hotly. But the other broke in quite as hotly.

"Pouf!—a fine protector, he! A wolf shielding the lambs! Whom has he protected? Has he not enslaved, has he not juggled with—has he not—"

"But, papa," Mademoiselle cried appealingly, "do I receive, or does Uncle Fauriel? Tell him he shall not spoil my day with his hateful politics. See, Monsieur Philip is very angry, and so am I."

The Keeper of the Archives laughed aloud. "Do not mind him, Monsieur the Page," he said; "this is a little pot and soon heated. There, there, Fauriel, do not get angry; you know your bark is worse than your bite. Let him alone; he is but a boy. What should he care for your tirades, except perhaps to love his Emperor the more and regard you the less?"

"But our boys are the Frenchmen of the future, Daunou," the little man replied. "I am angered to see them worshiping at the shrine of the Corsican—this Nicholas,[1] this little beast, this—"

"Sir!" Philip shouted.

"Uncle! Papa!" Mademoiselle protested. But, almost before he knew what he was doing, the angry page of the

[1] One of the Parisian nicknames of Napoleon.

PHILIP STRIKES UNCLE FAUKIEL.

palace sprang at the detractor of his Emperor and thumped him soundly on his ruffled shirt-front.

"Fellow!" he cried, red with rage, "he who maligns my Emperor insults me! Withdraw your words or I will kill you!"

But the fat calumniator of Napoleon looked into the face of the Emperor's young champion, and snapped his fingers once, twice, beneath the boy's nose.

"Pah! Infant!" he said. "That for you!" Then he turned his back on the angry boy and called out with the laugh that maddens, "Daunou, send for his nurse!"

CHAPTER VI

A FUSS WITH FOUCHÉ

PHILIP fairly cried with rage. A boy's wrath is sometimes so overmastering that it unnerves him, and he can do nothing but let it dissolve in tears. But the boy quickly dashed the unwelcome drops from his eyes, and turned to the Keeper of the Archives.

"Sir—" he began, but the Keeper interrupted him, gently but firmly:

"We are all citizens in this household, my boy," he said. "For us, at least, the Republic is not yet dead, nor have we grown weary of its simple ways."

"Citizen Keeper, then," Philip said, falling back upon the old address of the Revolution, "I bid you and Mademoiselle good day. If it be the ways of the Republic to malign the absent and to insult guests, then am I glad the Republic is dead. Long live the Emperor!"

And, deeply bowing, the boy turned toward the door. But the Keeper of the Archives caught him by the arm. "Amen to that wish, my son!" he said. "None surely could breathe it more sincerely than do I, though I neither countenance all the actions nor blindly follow the lead of the Emperor. I, too, am in the service of the State. So do I seek to render, as is my duty, loyal and devoted service, even though the Emperor does not love me, and I am friend enough to him to know his faults and wish him so well that I would see him mend them."

"And I am friend enough to Monsieur Philip—he, surely, is not yet old enough to be Citizen Philip, is he, papa?—to wish him well out of the nest of politics into which he has fallen." So said Mademoiselle. "For me, papa," she added, "I do think you might at least protect him from Uncle Fauriel here, whose tongue is sharper than Marcel's needle, without being able to do nearly as much work—nor as good, either."

Hereupon, Uncle Fauriel came forward, his hand extended, his fierceness lost in a smile.

"You are a brave boy, young Desnouettes," he said; "and I an old fool. My tongue is but a galloping steed that often bears me runaway. I ask your pardon. Any boy who has pluck enough to help the helpless and champion the absent has my admiration, even though the helpless one be the girl who detests her Uncle Fauriel, and the absent one be the Cor—the fellow I detest. Come, take both my apology and my hand. I need to fight with a fellow first to make me love him. And I love you. Here, friends all: a toast, in Mademoiselle's own grape-juice. I give you: 'Monsieur the Page! May Mademoiselle never need a doughtier knight, nor Napoleon himself a more loyal champion.' I drink to Monsieur the Page!"

And all the company caught up the delicate glasses from Mademoiselle's little table.

"To Monsieur the Page!" they cried, and emptied their glasses with a will.

"There, now; we are all friends, are we not?" cried Mademoiselle, gleefully. "Come, Monsieur Philip, let me finish papa's unlucky attempt. You must know us all." And, taking the boy's arm, the young girl introduced him to her guests.

The greetings were most cordial, and Philip soon found himself in such novel and yet such friendly surroundings that he was glad of the adventure, and even did not regret his quarrel. For even those who disagree with us think all the more of us if we are ready to defend our principles stoutly and with vigor. Philip's first principle was loyalty to the Emperor; and this he was prepared to maintain against all comers, and even in hostile company.

He enjoyed himself so much that he very nearly overstayed his time. His adieus, therefore, were hurried; but he accepted Citizen Daunou's earnest invitation to come to them again, and he bade Mademoiselle good day with boyish warmth and emphasis.

"I am so glad to have met you, Mademoiselle," he said, "that I do not even regret the fire."

"Nor I my ungracious flight from my preserver," she replied smilingly; "and — we yet may have that schottische."

As Philip was hurrying along the Street of the Fight toward the New Bridge, an arm was slipped through his, and a puffy, panting voice said, "So! but you travel fast, you boy. Let us walk together, we two."

It was Uncle Fauriel. Philip was almost startled by the friendliness of his late ferocious adversary.

"What! you, Monsieur?" he cried.

"Come, come; none of your aristocratic notions with me,

son of the *émigré*. Don't Monsieur me! I am plain Citizen Fauriel. That is surely enough for any honest Frenchman in these days, when marshals and dukes are as plenty as pease in a porridge; or you shall call me, as does my dear Mademoiselle — Uncle Fauriel. I should like to be Uncle to all the brave boys and girls of France. I wish to walk and talk with you, young Desnouettes. I meant nothing against you by my talk. Of course you know that. It is but my way. I hate the Corsican, and I make no secret of saying so — among friends."

"But why?" Philip inquired.

"Why?" Uncle Fauriel replied. "See here, my Philip; I am of the Revolution. I went through blood for the rights of man. I cried down kings and thrones. When that the abbey of St. Denis was sacked, I was there — to batter down its statues and dig up the bones of kings. I played foot-ball with the head of Henry of Navarre. I handed the red bonnet to Capet, and let loose toward heaven the doves of Robespierre. I sang 'Up, Vengeance!' with the loudest, and danced the Carmagnole with the maddest. Yes, I was not so fat then as to-day. I could dance. I adored the Revolution. I loved the Republic. But when the Republic became the Terror, and blood only was its soul, then I saw that even liberty can become tyranny, and longed for one who should save the nation. He came. It was the Corsican — the Commander, the Conqueror, the Consul. I hailed him as the deliverer of France. But power has puffed him up, and he who might have been France's savior is himself France's tyrant. Then I gave up — I who had been a soldier of the Republic, I who had served as secretary to Fouché —"

"The Duke of Otranto?" Philip cried in surprise.

"Give me no dukes, boy," Uncle Fauriel returned hotly. "He is but Fouché to me; and ever the same Fouché, though steeped in titles—Fouché, the renegade priest, bloodhound of the Terror, chief spy of the Empire!"

"Citizen!—quiet, quiet, I pray!" Philip exclaimed in alarm, but under his breath. "Fouché is everywhere."

"And you are a page of the Emperor," Uncle Fauriel said, with a knowing nod. "You are wise, you boy, and know upon which side of your bread the butter has been spread. But now you know why I hate the Corsican. He has betrayed liberty. I hailed him as the one man who might redeem France; he has been the one man to enslave her. So I gave up politics for pen-work. But still is my anger hot. Listen, son of the *émigré:* you are young; you are hopeful; you have everything to choose from and everything to do. Your life lies before you. Worship no man. If you must serve the Cor—the Emperor—then serve him well; not for his interest, though—for the nation's. Our boys are our only salvation. So, if I get growl-y, if I anger you again, forgive me and say to yourself: Uncle Fauriel is a madman; but he has run against all sorts of people and knows how small a thing is a man. Adieu, young Desnouettes; adieu, my Philip. Here is my home. You are a bright boy; be bright with both your eyes."

And with that the boy's new friend darted into the doorway of one of the lofty houses in the narrow Street of the Gibbet, leaving Philip wondering. So rapid had been Uncle Fauriel's flow of talk that Philip had not been able to get a word in edgewise. It was a new experience to him, to find men opposed to the Emperor—and not Austrians, nor Prussians, nor Englishmen, but Frenchmen! This gave him a sensation at once surprising and unpleasant. He could not understand it; for he saw that Uncle Fauriel, notwithstanding his hot temper, was a wise man. But at last, with a boy's ready carelessness, he threw aside the unpleasant notion even as he spurned the advice. "Hate the Emperor?" he said to himself. "How absurd! It is folly; it is treason!"

But, for all that, Philip's new friends proved such an attraction that the boy found his feet again and again turning down the narrow and peaceful Street of the Fight, and he became a welcome visitor at what her father, the Keeper of the Archives, was pleased to style, laughingly, "Mademoiselle's salon."

So it came about that, though Mademoiselle hated politics and Philip loved a good time, he could not help gathering much that was of value to an expanding young mind eager to hear and to learn of new and novel things. But besides much wise talk from the scholars and thinkers who frequented the house of the Keeper of the Archives, Philip also heard the tales related of what men had hoped and what men had done in the days when the Republic was really a dream of liberty; and how France might have been a second America if there could but have risen a Washington, as in the land beyond the sea. There, too, though he had many a war of words with "Uncle Fauriel," as he came to call him, Philip learned to love the fiery patriot who had hoped for so much, and had been so sadly disappointed, in the Revolution, the Republic, and the Consulate. For out

"'I AM HAPPY TO BE NEAR YOU, SIRE,' SAID PHILIP."

of these three had come the Empire; and to Uncle Fauriel the empire was only — the Corsican!

There are some natures that distrust makes all the more loyal. Such was Philip Desnouettes's. He redoubled his efforts to please this Emperor, whom some deemed more than mortal and some called less than man. He became so zealous in the doing of his duty that even Napoleon noticed his tireless energy, and, playfully pinching his ear, said to him one day in the Tuileries: "Don't hurry so, you boy. Time enough to overdo when occasion calls. I must keep young France healthy for France's needs. Help to make the palace bright and gay. Are you happy here, young Desnouettes?"

"I am happy to be near you, Sire," the boy replied. To which, with a smile and a nod, followed the imperial approval:

"Good boy"; and again came the favorite ear-pinching that every one about this singular man had experienced, from Empress and marshal down to page and post-boy. "And could you sing 'Zig-zag,' think you, as you did when you were our 'dirty boy,' for Uncle Bibiche and little Napoleon? Poor little Napoleon!"

For the little Prince Napoleon, the son of King Louis of Holland, the probable heir of his uncle the Emperor, had died suddenly in the days when Philip was at the school of St. Cyr. And no one had yet taken the bright little fellow's place in the Emperor's affections; for Napoleon had dearly loved his baby nephew and namesake.

The very day of the recognition of Philip's zeal by the Emperor was also one of Mademoiselle's "salon days," and Philip's exuberance of spirits found vent in a particularly hot debate with Uncle Fauriel, who delighted to stir the boy's loyalty into fresh protestations.

Even during their roundabout walk homeward from the Street of the Fight, by way of the Square of the Louvre, they still kept up the talk, and both grew so heated over it that Uncle Fauriel was glad to stop a lemonade-man and "stand treat" in some of the acid coolness that the man drew for them from the odd-looking tank he carried on his back.

As they turned to cross the square, Uncle Fauriel, occupied in wiping the moisture from his lips, was well nigh run over by a coach which came dashing heedlessly across their path, and was saved from the collision only by Philip's strong young hand.

"Now then, stupid one! What are eyes for, you?" cried the coachman, scarcely deigning to rein up his horses at this narrow escape.

"Ah, beast!" Uncle Fauriel called back, furiously. "If I but had here you and your master, I would teach you manners!" and he shook his fist at horses and driver as the coach rolled past. The man within, attracted by the jar and the loud voices, looked out at the window. He caught sight of Uncle Fauriel's doubled fist; he saw the protecting arm of the page. A decoration gleamed upon his breast; a look of mingled recognition and contempt was on his heavy face.

And, as that face appeared at the window, Uncle Fauriel only shook his fist the harder. "Ah, you spy!" he cried; "you would run down honester men than yourself, would you?"

But Philip, too, had recognized the heavy face at the coach window.

UNCLE FAURIEL SHAKES HIS FIST AT FOUCHÉ.

"My faith!" he exclaimed, as he dragged Uncle Fauriel away; "but you will get yourself into trouble, Citizen Uncle, with that tongue of yours. Did you see who it was, that?"

"Did I not, then?" was the reply. "Bah! the spy!" And again he shook his fist at the retreating carriage. The man within the coach was Fouché, the Emperor's hated chief of police.

The next day, as Philip was awaiting orders at the Tuileries, an order came. "Young Desnouettes is called to the Emperor," cried the first page, Malvirade. And Philip passed into the Emperor's study.

"So, sir, you consort with malcontents, do you? You conspire with traitors, eh?" the Emperor broke out, even before the page could make his salute. "Is this, then, your return for my good offices?"

The tone was so different from the imperial greeting of the day before, it was so startling in its hostility, that Philip drew back in surprise; dismayed and dumfounded, he was unable to reply.

"What! have you no tongue, you boy?" the Emperor cried. "Come! speak! Speak up, you!"

"Sire," stammered the boy, "I do not know what you mean. I—" Then the words came with the ring of sincerity—"Some one has spoken falsely. No one loves or serves you more faithfully than I."

"So! we boast, do we?" the Emperor almost snarled. "'T is a false service, though. I know your ways better than you think. What plots are you conspiring with Fauriel, who hates me? What takes you so often to the house of that Daunou? What would these treason-workers have of you—of you, a page of the Emperor? Is your *émigré* blood telling, after all? Are you the cat's-paw to pull out the chestnuts?"

"Sire," Philip said proudly, "my father was faithful unto death. My friends are no traitors."

"Are they not, then? How is it, Otranto? What enlightening can you give this young fool who protests and prates so glibly?" And Napoleon turned toward one who, till now, had kept in shadow.

Then Philip recognized and remembered. His accuser was Fouché, who never deemed any one too high nor any one too low for his schemings—Fouché, Duke of Otranto, and minister of police.

"Did not I see you in the Square of the Louvre but yesterday with the Citizen Fauriel, as he calls himself—Fauriel, the loudest-mouthed foe to the Emperor in all Paris?" the minister of police inquired in his cool, exasperating way. "Have you not again and again visited the house of Daunou, Keeper of the Archives, who lives in the Street of the Fight—Daunou, the Emperor's most inveterate opponent?"

"I have no cause to deny my friendships, Monsieur the Duke," Philip replied calmly.

"But are these friendships for a page of the Emperor?" Fouché inquired. "And does not that malcontent Fauriel,—my secretary once, remember,—does he not attack the Emperor openly? Did he not, yesterday, shake his fist at me, the Emperor's representative, in the public streets?"

"He did, Monsieur the Duke," Philip admitted frankly. "But it was not from enmity, that. It was but his way, as you—"

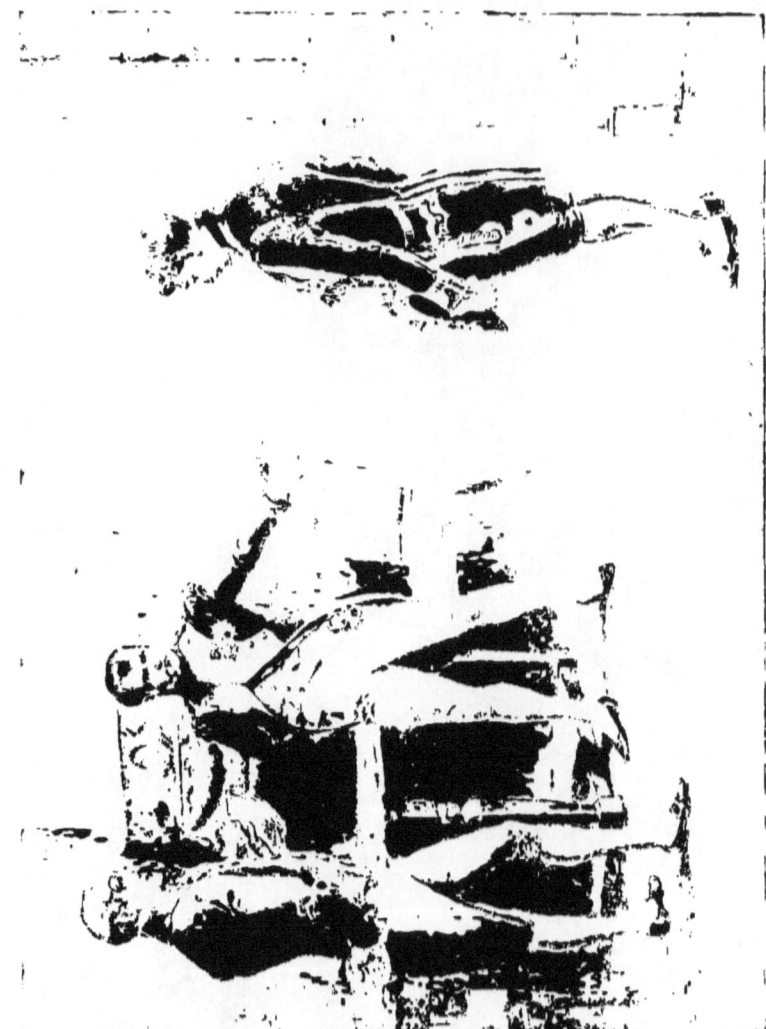

"'GO! YOU ARE DISMISSED FROM THE SERVICE OF THE EMPEROR!'"

"Bah! His way! his way!" the Emperor broke in. "Then is not his way ours. Look, you page; I can have no divided duty, no questionable loyalty, in those who are of my household. You have chosen to consort with malcontents; you take your friends from among my enemies; you shall not, then, serve me. Go! You are dismissed from the service of the Emperor!"

CHAPTER VII

THE MISSION OF CITIZEN DAUNOU

CITIZEN DAUNOU sat in his office in the palace of the Prince of Soubise—palace and prince no longer, however; for the splendid old mansion in the Rue du Chaume,—or, as we should say, the Street of the Wheatfield,—with its gardens, its courts, and its arcades, had been confiscated by the Republic, while its princely owners were fugitives from their home-land, fighting "the Corsican" in the armies of the foes of France.

The old palace was now the Bureau of Archives, the building in which were kept the public papers of the Empire. And here, surrounded by dusty documents, curious chronicles, and ancient records, sat the Keeper of the Archives, the citizen Pierre Daunou. His windows looked out upon the horseshoe-like Court of the Princes and the pillared porticos that encircled the garden. A pile of papers was heaped upon his desk—maps, title-deeds, confiscation records, and schedules of property taken by the Emperor from the conquered countries of Europe that were now dependencies or vassals of the Empire.

Some of these papers were of rare historic value; some told, by their very presence in that place, sad stories of persecution, dispossession, defeat, and loss.

The scholarly old Keeper was so immersed in his study of one of these "genealogic finds" that he did not hear the little tap for admission, nor the stealthy invasion of his sanctum that followed close upon the tap, until two soft hands imprisoned his eyes. Then, drawing the hands away, he looked up and saw something much more attractive than parchments or confiscation records. It was Mademoiselle.

"So; it is you, truant, is it?" he cried gaily. "And who—why—live the people! it is Page Philip! Is not that now the most singular chance? Here was I just thinking of you—just reading the name of Desnouettes. Let me tell you—but—eh?—holo, boy! What gloomy faces! Why, girl, what is the trouble, you two? Is something wrong at home?"

"Not at our home, papa," Mademoiselle replied; "and Philip has none."

"Has none? What is all this?"

"The Emperor has dismissed me from his service, Citizen Daunou," Philip replied.

"But why?"

"Why," Philip said hesitatingly, "because—some one has lied to him. Because—"

"Because, papa, we are his friends," Mademoiselle declared.

"Because of us? No; but is it so, Philip?" Citizen Daunou demanded, as if incredulous. "Has, then, your friendship with my house brought you to grief? Tell me; tell me, boy."

Then Philip told the story of his disgrace. He declared, too, that the dismissal was so sudden and bewildering that he had made neither plea nor protest in reply, but had simply withdrawn from the palace, and, quite dazed by the blow, had wandered about the streets until his feet had instinctively turned down the Street of the Fight. Instinctively, too, he had entered the house of his friends, and there he had found Mademoiselle and quick sympathy. For thus unloading his woes on his friends he asked Citizen Daunou's pardon, but—

"My pardon?" the old man exclaimed. "Why, Philip boy, I ought rather to ask it of you. You do but suffer for me—for us."

"There! That is what I told Philip, papa," Mademoiselle cried triumphantly; "and straightway dragged him here—an unwilling captive. I told him you would see him righted."

"See him righted—I? I see him—Why!—one moment, you! There, there; let me think. So—eh—why, of course! Come; run home, you young folks, and let me think it out—let me think it—death of my life! but I see a light."

"But, Citizen," Philip began, "I ought not—"

"Will you obey me, Philip, and vanish—you and Mademoiselle there?" the Keeper of the Archives said, almost forcing them from the room. "How can I think if you children stay here—chatter, chatter, chatter? Out on you, miscreants!—blocking all work in the public offices. Come; go, go!—go home, and do not fret until I tell you to."

"My faith, though! Is he not a terrible old mustache, Philip?" Mademoiselle cried, in mock terror. "Come, let us be gone before he eats us both—this ogre in his castle, here. I told you he could manage it all—you wise old papa!" Here she dismayed the "ogre" with a rush, a hug, and a kiss. "Come you, Philip; let us go and see Babette."

"Yes; go anywhere, anywhere, giddy ones," said the Keeper of the Archives. "Go and see Babette. Ah! stop yet. This Babette, Philip—" here he looked at the parchment on his desk once more—"is she, perhaps, your sister?"

"My sister? Babette?" Philip replied. "My faith! I think not, Citizen Daunou. She is Mother Thérèse's daughter; or so I have always thought."

"You do not know, though, eh?" Citizen Daunou said. "Is she—is she—" here he looked at the document again— "is she of your age?"

"My age? Oh, no, Citizen," Philip answered, with the laugh of superiority. "Why! I am fourteen, and as for Babette—Babette is barely ten."

"Ah, so? That is bad; that is—well, well—I was only curious. There, there, run along; such chatterers, you two! Wasting the Emperor's time!"

"And again we are chatterers, Philip! But what then is Monsieur the Keeper of the Archives? Come away, Philip; he is dangerous. Good day, ogre!" and the laughing Mademoiselle dragged the ex-page from the room.

For a full half hour after the young people had left him, Citizen Daunou sat at his desk, studying the paper that lay open before him, and thinking intently. Then, rising, he drew on his long street-coat, thrust the paper in his pocket, flung his chapeau on his head, and, hailing a cab at the door of the Bureau of Archives, drove straight to the Tuileries.

Meantime, Philip and Mademoiselle had given up their

plan of calling upon Babette, because it was not visitors' day at the convent school. So they had wandered up the dirty Street of St. Denis, swarming with people. They strolled along the boulevards, stopping now to watch and wonder at a juggler's free show on the street, now to pity and pay the baby tambourine-player by the rising walls of the new Exchange, or now to watch the boys at a game of prisoners' base in the Place Vendôme. Then, after planning an afternoon picnic in the Boulogne woods, Mademoiselle was left at the house in the Street of the Fight, to which Philip was to return when he had executed her commissions at certain of the shops in the Palace Royal.

As for his troubles, they did not worry Philip overmuch. From despair he had been raised to hope, for he had faith in Citizen Daunou; and then, too, he was a boy—and boys cast off such troubles easily.

As he made his way toward the Palace Royal and was crossing the new and splendid Street of Rivoli, there fell on his ears a sharp order of the police:

"Aside there; way for the Empress!"

Philip saw the dashing outriders, the mounted escort, and then the open carriage drawn by four horses. He recognized the Empress sitting smiling within, and, as the imperial carriage rolled past, Philip, true to his old custom, drew up and saluted the Empress. She saw him, and, turning, suddenly beckoned him to her side. Philip, still acting according to custom, ran alongside and, hat in hand, sprang to the step of the carriage, which did not even need to slacken its speed for him.

"It is you, Page Desnouettes? Go to the Emperor. Tell

PHILIP RIDES ON THE STEP OF THE EMPRESS'S CARRIAGE.

him I have changed my mind, and drive to the Little Trianon instead of St. Cloud. Bid him meet me there this afternoon." Thus ran the commands of the Empress to the page.

"But, your Majesty—" Philip began.

"How, boy!" cried the young Empress; "'but' to me? What would you say? Are you on service in another direction?"

"Alas! your Majesty," Philip sadly replied, "I am on no service at all; nor can I be. I am no longer page. I—I—have been dismissed."

"Dismissed? You—my good page?" the Empress exclaimed. "But why? Ah, Madame the Countess, would you permit the page to enter? I wish to question him. So; many thanks. Now tell me the story, Page Desnouettes."

And so it came to pass that the disgraced page drove along the Street of Rivoli in the carriage of the Empress.

Frankly and briefly he told the story.

"Ah, that terrible ball! And you saved the girl; and her father is grateful to you? And he is Keeper of the Archives? How can he then be untrue to the Emperor he serves? And it was Fouché who brought you to grief? Ah, that Fouché—I do not like him overmuch"; this, half to herself. Then she said: "And it is not true, is it, you boy? You are no enemy to the Emperor?"

"Madame—your Majesty, I would die for him," Philip declared.

"I knew it. You shall live for him," the Empress said. "Here, lend me your tablets. So!" And she dashed off a hurried line. "This to the Emperor. If that does not answer, I will see him myself. Why, you once saved his life, so he said. Now we must save you. There, begone, young Desnouettes. I am your friend. And do not forget my own message to the Emperor. This afternoon at the Little Trianon."

The gracious young Empress gave the page her hand to kiss. The page clambered to the carriage-step, saluted his mistress, and sprang nimbly to the street, while the Empress and her escort sped on to Versailles and the beautiful Trianon, eleven miles away.

"Two good friends for me," Philip pleased himself with thinking as he hurried back to the Tuileries. "You are in luck, you page."

In the study of the Emperor the Keeper of the Archives had gained an audience with Napoleon.

"Ah, Monsieur Daunou,— pardon me,"—this a bit sarcastically,—"*Citizen* Daunou,—you are welcome. Foes as well as friends may be welcomed, may they not, Citizen?"

"I trust, Sire, your Majesty does not count me among your foes," Citizen Daunou said.

"Well, call it opponents then," the Emperor replied. "But—I believe you, sir, are a faithful servant of the Empire, even though you do decline my gifts and gather my opponents under your roof. What is your pleasure?"

"I come, Sire, to expiate a crime," Citizen Daunou asserted.

"So; it has come to that, has it?" Napoleon declared. "You regret these gatherings, then, do you?"

"I regret, Sire, that they are deemed unfriendly by you," replied the Keeper of the Archives. "Whoever has asserted that they are disloyal is no friend to the truth. But even such friendly reunions as these gatherings have seriously injured in your Majesty's eyes one who is your Majesty's most devoted servant and most outspoken champion."

"Meaning yourself, Citizen Keeper?"

"I mean young Philip Desnouettes, Sire."

"Ha! that boy?"

"Yes, Sire. He saved my dear little daughter that fearful night at the Embassy ball," the Keeper of the Archives explained. "My heart and home have been free to him ever since. It seems my love for the lad has worked his ruin. Sire, I plead for his recall."

"So! He has been whining to you of my displeasure?" the Emperor exclaimed.

"Sire, young Desnouettes never whines. He is too manly a lad — too devoted to you, for that. I heard of his trouble against his will. I ask his recall, not only as an act of justice, such as your Majesty is ever willing to do, but as the payment of a debt which I well know your Majesty will not repudiate."

"How? A debt?" the Emperor said. "What is it you mean, sir?"

"This, Sire." And the Keeper of the Archives drew from his pocket the document he had placed there. "Singularly enough," he said, "just at the moment the lad was brought to me I was reading here his name — or rather that of his father."

"The *émigré* Desnouettes?"

"Yes, Sire—the *émigré*, and your prophet."

"My prophet!" The Emperor looked at the Keeper in wonderment. "You speak in riddles, sir."

"No riddle, Sire, but a plain and recorded fact," replied the Keeper. "Permit me. Here is the deed of confiscation recorded against the estates of the suspected Citizen Augustin Desnouettes of Riom, executed for contempt of the decrees of the Directory in May, 1796. Here, attached to it, are the minutes of his trial. In these it appears that the Suspect, Citizen Augustin Desnouettes, lost his head for prophesying that the only savior of France would be General Bonaparte."

"How, sir? Is this the fact?"

"Listen, Sire." And the Keeper of the Archives read from the minutes:

"And the said Suspect, the *émigré* Augustin Desnouettes, did, of his own motion, seek to cast discredit upon the Directory by maintaining that it was powerless to save France from disruption, and that the only salvation for the Republic lay in the success of Citizen General Bonaparte, for whose welfare he devoutly prayed, and to whose kind remembrance he confided the future of his motherless children—"

"His children? There was but this boy," the Emperor said.

"So I thought, Sire; but here is the record:

'—his motherless children, who would be left orphans by their father's death.'

"'THERE WAS BUT THIS BOY,' THE EMPEROR SAID."

"And here, appended to the deed, is this minute:

'By order of the Directory the twin children of the *émigré* Augustin Desnouettes are to be bound over to the Citizen Jules Rapin, of the Street of the Washerwomen, in the Fourth Ward of Paris, and to the Cit—'

"Here, Sire, the record ends, for the rest is missing."

The Emperor took the paper and examined it minutely.

"Bah, the incapables!" he said at last. "How heedless those fellows were under that sheep-like Directory! To file papers so carelessly! See; it has been torn off."

"So I think, Sire,—either carelessly or for a purpose," the Keeper of the Archives said.

"Twin children," mused Napoleon. "Then where is the other? And was it boy or girl?"

"That, Sire, I too would know."

"See to it; see to it, Citizen Daunou," the Emperor commanded. "It is work for such a shrewd searcher as you. Ferret out the mystery, and let me know. I, too, would— Well, sir, what is this?" For at that moment the First Page, Malvirade, handed him a folded paper. "From the Empress?" Then he opened the slip, read it, frowned, laughed, and handed it to the Keeper of the Archives. "See: it rains pleas for young Desnouettes! Read it, Daunou."

And Citizen Daunou read with surprise, in the handwriting of the Empress: "For my sake recall Page Desnouettes. He is my chosen page, you remember. LOUISE."

"With so powerful an advocate, Sire," the Keeper of the Archives said, "my words are not needed."

"The Empress has her way, generally," Napoleon said. "Who brought this, Malvirade?"

"Page Desnouettes, Sire," the First Page replied. "And also a verbal message from the Empress."

"Bid him enter—or no; wait without until I summon you. Then to the Keeper the Emperor said: "I was perhaps hasty, Daunou—hasty and worried, I think, with weightier matters. I like the boy, too; but Fouché—ah, well! Fouché is not always to be depended upon. I will see to the lad's recall. And, come, my friend: think better of the Emperor. Believe that I, too, would serve France quite as sincerely—yes, more sincerely—than even you stern old relics of the Revolution, who can see no further than the glorious days of '92."

And, rising, the Emperor laid his hand almost affectionately on Daunou's shoulder.

"Sire," the stout old republican responded, "my service and loyalty go together. I serve you as Keeper of the Archives. In that service I trust you will believe that duty and loyalty go hand in hand."

"I believe you, Daunou; I believe you!" the Emperor replied; "though I know you do not love my methods. Be loyal still. Serve France. And I am France!"

Citizen Daunou found it hard to rein in his protest at this imperial announcement. But he bowed in adieu, saying nothing. And the Emperor added: "Trace up the other child of the *émigré* Desnouettes, my friend. That mystery must be unraveled. I, who would be just to my foes, must be generous to my friends. This Desnouettes, it would appear, almost died for me. His son must be my charge.

But, silence in this matter, my friend, until something is reached. Let me know of your progress. The best of luck to your hunting!"

The Keeper of the Archives left, and the page was summoned.

"So, rascal!" the Emperor said, stern of eye and voice, "you go about complaining, do you? You work on the sympathies of both republican and Empress, eh?"

"No, Sire," Philip replied; "I sought neither. But Citizen Daunou learned of my dismissal, and the Empress stopped me in the street to bid me take a message to your Majesty; and thus she, too, learned my story."

"Well, sir; her message."

Philip delivered it.

"Little Trianon, eh?" Napoleon said. "Very well; and you, sir, make ready to attend me there."

"As page—or—prisoner, Sire?" the boy queried.

"You young monkey!" And the Emperor pulled Philip's hair roughly, but in token of good humor. "As page, I suppose, since my will is thus openly set at naught. And see that you do good service, you page."

"And—am I debarred from visiting my friends, Sire?" the boy persisted.

"What! When you champion my cause so roundly in the very camp of the enemy?" replied the Emperor. "No, no, you boy; I make you—see, 't is a good creation!—Hereditary Champion to the Emperor! See to it, young Desnouettes, that, as it was in the knightly days, my champion is fearless, loyal, brave, and true. Now, go; report your recall to Malvirade, and in two hours attend me to the Trianon."

Philip kissed the Emperor's hand joyfully, and ten minutes later was working off his surplus spirits by playing leap-frog up and down the corridor with six spry young pages. Then, in his most lordly style, he despatched one of the porters of the palace in haste to the Street of the Fight, bearing a message of regret to Mademoiselle, that "a special engagement with the Emperor" would make it necessary to defer the pleasure of a picnic in the Boulogne woods until a more convenient season.

CHAPTER VIII

THE "COURIER OF THE KING"

THE trip to the Trianon was a red-letter day for Philip. The English garden, the Swiss village, and the little theater, forever associated with the sad story of Marie Antoinette, were new and agreeable sights for this boy, who had open eyes for everything.

The Emperor was gracious, and even gay; the Empress had a kind word for the boy she had not forgotten; and Philip, quick to cast sorrow aside, enjoyed the passing moment, attended faithfully upon his imperial patrons, and yet managed to "take in" all the sights that have made forever famous this celebrated "annex" to the splendid palace of Versailles.

The days flew by. Philip did remember his dismissal and reinstatement sufficiently to stir himself up to such a desire to show his gratitude to the Emperor and Empress, that Citizen Daunou cautioned him against over-exertion; and Uncle Fauriel, who was less vituperative after he found how nearly he had brought the boy into trouble, nevertheless declared that Philip was fairly running his legs off for "the Corsican," and stated his intention of applying at the palace for the position of Philip's substitute, so that he might work off some of his superfluous flesh, whereat everyone laughed.

The picnic in the Boulogne woods came about in due time. Babette was there, and so, too, were Citizen Daunou and Uncle Fauriel. And whom should the children meet in their wanderings in the woods, but the Emperor and Empress, walking about like any "goodman and his wife," and not close hedged by all the state and escort that usually environed them in their "outings" around Paris.

They recognized Philip, and stopped to speak with the children. The Emperor questioned Babette about her schooling, and had something kindly to say to Mademoiselle about her escape from the Embassy; he pinched and petted the little girls, and rumpled all the order and dignity out of Philip's yellow locks, until Babette lost her timidity and laughed aloud at the imperial pranks, while Mademoiselle was so charmed with both the "royalties" that, after hearing her enthusiastic talk, Uncle Fauriel declared the house in the Street of the Fight would be contaminated by her "imperialism," and vowed that he would have to desert it for some red republican gathering in the St. Denis quarter, or consort with the only real haters of "the Corsican"— the Bourbon exiles beyond the Rhine.

Autumn passed, and winter came. Fouché was in disgrace. He had been deposed from his position as Minister of Police for concocting secret measures contrary to the Emperor's will. But Philip, not being specially interested in political plots and moves, was sure that this was *his* revenge, and boasted to Uncle Fauriel that the great Minister of Police had fallen because he had sought to set the Emperor against the page.

"Piff, pouf!" puffed Uncle Fauriel; "hear our cockerel crow! Of course it was so. When does your Excellency look for the portfolio of the Minister of Police to be offered you, as Fouché's successor?"

"Minister of Police!" Mademoiselle exclaimed; "Philip would n't look at that position. He will be—what do you call it?—the Arch-Chancellor himself some fine day; and then, be sure, he will banish you, Uncle Fauriel, for talking treason against the Emperor; and he will order the Imperial Guard to lead you in chains to the barrier, or else have you condemned to stand on one leg on the top of the Vendome Column and shout, 'Long live the Emperor!' until you are hoarse."

March came in that eventful year of 1811; and when the morning of the twentieth dawned all Paris was in the streets. For like wildfire spread the rumor: there is a baby at the Tuileries! Every hour the crowd grew denser. At open windows, along the streets, in the great garden of the Tuileries, people waited expectant, listening for the voice of the cannons of the Invalid Soldiers' Home to tell whether the baby was a boy or a girl. Of course every one hoped it was a boy; for that meant an heir to the throne of France—their future Emperor.

At the first boom a mighty silence fell upon the listening city. Every one stopped, intent, anxious. One—two—three, they counted. Boom, boom! went the guns up to nineteen—twenty—twenty-one. The silence was intense, the anxiety profound. Twenty-two! There came a mighty cheer, a roar from thousands and thousands of throats. Hats were flung aloft; people cried with joy, and danced and hugged each other, and cared no more to count, though the guns boomed away until the full salute of one hundred and one was fired. For that twenty-second boom told the story. Twenty-one guns meant a girl. One hundred and one were for a boy. No need to count after the twenty-second boom! The baby at the Tuileries was a boy.

Then, out of the cheering, came the mighty shout: "Long live the Emperor! Long live the Empress! Long live the King of Rome!" For that was to be the title of this baby prince, whose mother was an empress, whose father was ruler over kings.

Philip was in the palace, busy enough. He, too, at the twenty-second gun — though he of course had already heard the truth — felt the inspiration of excitement, and although he was in the precincts of the palace could, like "the ranks of Tuscany" in Macaulay's famous ballad,

"— scarce forbear to cheer."

But he did not. A page of the palace, on duty, must be quiet and circumspect. So Philip reined in his enthusiasm, and, even before the echo of the one hundred and first gun had died away, he was holding aside the curtains which fell before the doorway that opened into the Blue Room. A short, stout man passed hurriedly between the parted curtains. In his arms he bore a precious bundle swathed in richest robes. This man was the Emperor.

"Gentlemen," he said to the assembled dignitaries who awaited in the Blue Room the official tidings, "I present to you the King of Rome!"

Down upon one knee, in homage to the imperial baby,

"'I PRESENT TO YOU THE KING OF ROME!'"

dropped each man in that glittering throng of soldiers and statesmen. And as the little King of Rome lifted his voice in a wail of welcome, or, perhaps, of protest, there came from the kneeling throng the triple shout of loyalty and reverence: "Long live the Emperor! Long live the Empress! Long live the King of Rome!"

All day Paris was in a fever of joy. What they had

wished for had happened. An heir to the throne had been born. The semaphore, or signal-telegraph, flashed the news from city on to city; fast-riding couriers, pages, and messengers bore the official announcement to distant municipalities and foreign courts; the people absolutely lived in the streets, talking over the event on corner and curb, on boulevard and in café. From a great balloon, that went up from the Field of Mars, papers were flung out to the people in commemoration of the notable event, and a constantly shifting crowd thronged the garden of the Tuileries, satisfied simply to gaze upon the palace that held the heir to the Empire.

The Emperor overflowed with joy. He could not keep still. He wandered from cradle to cabinet, now looking at his son, now looking at his people; and he who was unmoved by victory on the battle-field, and accustomed to every form of popularity and adoration, felt the pride of a father overtop the dignity of a king. As he looked at the great crowd in the garden, as he heard the bells pealing joyfully from every church-tower and the guns thundering in salute, tears of thankfulness and joy streamed down his cheeks. For the day on which his son was born was, beyond all question, Napoleon's happiest day.

In the evening the baby Prince was privately christened in the chapel of the Tuileries, and to him was given the sounding name of Francis Charles Joseph Napoleon, King of Rome and Heir of France.

Every house in the city, palace and hovel and lofty apartment-house alike, was brilliantly illuminated; fireworks flashed and whirled in every public square; while on the river that wound in and out, spanned by its dozen bridges, the Seine boatmen celebrated the birth of the little King by an impromptu river parade, sparkling with lights and crowned with show and song.

Philip was a tired boy when night came, for this had been a busy day. But as, after delivering a message to the Emperor, he paused for a moment to look at the imperial baby asleep in its costly cradle of mother-of-pearl and gold, above which, as if in protection, hovered a winged figure of Victory, the Emperor turned to him and said: "Young Desnouettes, I intrust you with a special duty. To-morrow you shall bear to the Empress Josephine a letter announcing the birth of my son. You shall travel not as a page of the palace, but as a courier of the King."

Here was an honor! The boy could scarcely sleep for excitement, anticipation, and joy. The next morning found him waiting, eager for the start; and before noon he was speeding across the country, a special courier, bearing the important tidings to the ex-Empress Josephine, who was then at her castle of Navarre, in Normandy, forty miles away.

What a ride it was! The day was clear and bright—early spring in France. Through the streets of the city, still echoing with the joyous festivities of the day before, the boy rode from the Tuileries, in a light canopy-carriage known as a gondola calash. It was drawn by four spirited horses; a postilion in imperial livery rode one of each pair of horses, and there was an equerry on the box.

Over the Seine and out into the open country, along the highroad that led to Évreux, the swift conveyance dashed, with the right of way on all the route, changing horses every ten miles, while the postilion's horn rang out the warning of approach, and the cry "In the name of the Emperor!" kept the highway clear. In town and village and from quaint little roadside homes throngs came out to stare and shout and cheer, for all the people recognized the imperial livery, and knew that the boy in the carriage was a royal page riding on the Emperor's service.

Night was shutting down as, past the scattered lights of Évreux town, Philip rode into the forest shadows, through which gleamed at last the lights of the royal château.

The calash drew up at the door; the boy alighted, and then, ascending the steps between a double file of flickering torches held by light-bearers, Philip, the Courier of the King of Rome, entered the palace.

He felt as important as if he were the Emperor himself. And yet, what do you suppose he was thinking? "My faith! don't I wish that pig of a Pierre, who used to call me 'mud prince' when I lived in the Street of the Washerwomen, could see me now! Would n't his eyes stick out, though? I am as good as a prince, I am. Room for the Courier of the King!"

This, however, was but the thought of an instant. He was really impressed with his mission, and anxious to deliver his message worthily and well.

He bowed to the majordomo who received him. "From the Emperor," he said; "a message to her Majesty. In haste."

With a formal bow, but with a half wink and a twinkle of the eye as he "sized up" this youthful bit of importance, the majordomo ushered the courier into the reception-room,

THE "COURIER OF THE KING."

and despatched a page to announce his arrival to the Empress.

The summons soon came: "Admit the messenger from the Emperor." And Philip passed on.

In the chief salon (or reception-room) of this small palace of Navarre, Josephine awaited the messenger from the court. Once an Empress, and wife to the Emperor, she still, though separated from him by the cruel necessities of state policy and the imperial succession, held his honor and esteem. By her side sat her guest of renown, Prince Eugene Beauharnais, Viceroy of Italy, her dearly loved son, while around her were grouped the ladies and gentlemen of her court.

At a signal, the doors of the salon were flung open; the Master of Ceremonies announced, "From the Emperor!" Then, in his imperial livery of crimson, green, and gold, plentifully sprinkled with the imperial bees; with his light-green shoulder-knot and streamers fringed with gold and stamped with the eagle and the "N"; in his hand his black-and-gold chapeau, decorated with its tricolor cockade and lined with white feathers—enter Philip the page!

Josephine greeted him with the gracious smile that won so many to her side.

"It is young Desnouettes, is it not?" she said.

"Yes, your Majesty," Philip replied, bowing low.

"I remember you well," said the Empress. "It was you—was it not?—with whom my grandson, poor little Prince Napoleon, once had so good a time under the chestnut-trees of St. Cloud?"

"Yes, your Majesty," Philip replied, all the time struggling to detach his letter from beneath his crimson vest, where he had stowed it for greater security.

Poor boy! He had fastened the Emperor's letter too securely. He tugged, and worked, and grew very red in the face, thinking all the time, "What a fool I was not to have taken it out while I was waiting below!"

But the Empress, true to her kindly nature, seemed not to notice the boy's discomfiture, and talked steadily to him as he worked. At last the note was detached, and, dropping upon his knee, the boy presented it to the Empress.

"From the Emperor, your Majesty," he said.

Josephine took the letter eagerly, and accompanied by her son, Prince Eugene, withdrew to read it, while Philip, left in the saloon, was the center of attraction, and gave a glowing account of the festivities in Paris. But when the ladies asked eagerly how the little King looked, Philip stammered, rubbed his ear, and said, "Oh, I don't know. The cradle is beautiful, and it is true he is fine—but, my faith! so small—and so red!"

When the Empress returned, she too talked with the boy. Then came dancing and games and general conversation, in all of which Philip was included as an especial guest, and did have "such a good time"!

Tea was served at eleven, after which the Empress retired. But first she sent for Philip, and gave him a letter. "This for the Emperor," she said; and added, with a merry twinkle in her eye, "Keep it as safe and secure as you kept the other." Then she handed him a packet. "This for yourself," she said, "as one who bore good tidings. You will be going early in the morning, young Desnouettes. Thank you for your faithful duty. I shall report it to the Emperor. Be a loyal page, my boy. Serve the Emperor faithfully; so shall you best serve France."

Philip kissed her extended hand, bowed, and retired. But, before he slept, his eager hands opened the parcel. He started with surprise and joy. The Empress had given "the bearer of good tidings" a splendid diamond hat-buckle, worth, so we are assured by the record, fully a thousand dollars.

Philip was wild with delight; for he dearly loved beautiful things.

He was up and away early the next morning, delighted with his reception, proud of his success, and more than ever in love with the kind-hearted and unfortunate lady whom men still called the Empress Josephine.

Merrily his relays of horses hurried his light calash over the highway. Through town and village, as before, he rode in haste,—"In the name of the Emperor!" giving him the right of way. But when he reached St. Germain, he found himself ahead of schedule time, and bade the equerry direct the postilions to change the route, and, crossing the Seine, swing around so as to enter Paris by the St. Denis gate. Across country to St. Denis he rode, and, passing beneath the noble arch that spanned the gate, he entered the city.

Philip felt like a conqueror making a royal progress as he rode down the long and dirty Street of St. Denis—the Bowery of old Paris. Street boys hailed him with cheers: venders offered him their wares, from waffles to hot potatoes; people stopped and stared; and still he had the right of way.

Then a great desire filled the boy's heart. He would go to the palace by the way of the Street of the Washerwomen. That would make the triumph of his trip complete. The people of the quarter should see that the mud prince had become a real prince. If only now "that pig of a Pierre" could see him!

So, obedient to his instructions, the postilions turned off from the Street of St. Denis into the Street of the Needlemakers, and thence into the Street of the Washerwomen. The well-remembered street of his boyhood was but a narrow thoroughfare, scarcely twelve feet wide, with barely room for two carriages to pass each other.

It was as dirty as ever, and so were its people. And what a shout they raised as the imperial carriage whirled along the narrow street! Pigs scampered, children scattered, dogs barked, and on rode Philip like a prince in state.

But, alas! pride goes before a fall. Just before he reached the fountain which was at once the scene and monument of his famous fight with "that pig of a Pierre," bang! went the carriage against some unseen obstacle; off flew the wheel; and, out of the carriage where he rode in state, went the Courier of the King—head first into the dirty street! The crowd rushed to the rescue. Officious hands picked up the prostrate page, and brushed from his fine clothes the mud of the Street of the Washerwomen. The wheel was readjusted; the boy took his seat again, angry and crestfallen; the postilions started their horses. But when, suddenly thinking of his mission, Philip clapped a hand to his pocket to make sure that the letter and the buckle were safe, a cold sweat broke out all over the startled page. Frantically he prodded himself in every spot; feverishly he felt in every pocket. It was all to no purpose. The letter and the diamond buckle both were missing!

CHAPTER IX

"THAT PIG OF A PIERRE"

"STOP, you! Tell them to stop, Etienne! I have lost my letter!"

Philip's voice rang out so strained and startled that Etienne, the equerry, turned about with a jerk, and the postilions reined up so quickly that the horses were almost thrown upon their haunches.

Back to the fountain raced page and equerry, their eyes upon the muddy roadway. At their coming, the crowd quickly gathered again, and though Etienne, the equerry, threw all possible authority into his command, "In the name of the Emperor!" it did not suffice to keep the crowd at bay, nor to scatter the swarm of over-zealous street-boys, who, under the pretense of hunting, only confused things all the more. And, not content with poking the mud, they indulged their bent in poking fun at the unfortunates so openly that Etienne, the equerry, stamped with rage, and Philip's flushed face showed how keenly these street jokes cut.

The search was fruitless. Half distracted, Philip was turning away, when there pushed through the crowd a stoutly built young fellow of sixteen. He wore a sort of half uniform, and had in his walk just a bit of swagger, like that of one who, now and then, was favored with a little brief authority.

He looked searchingly at the page an instant; then he pushed forward.

"By the candle that hung the baker!" he cried, "it's the 'prince'! You are young Desnouettes, you;—he who lived with Mother Thérèse, and is now page of the palace—is it not so? What is wrong with you?"

Philip greeted anything that looked like help. There was a certain amount of interest in the boy's tone, and the page, like a drowning man, was ready to clutch at any straw.

"We were upset here. I was thrown out, and have lost a letter meant for the palace."

"Bad enough! Bad enough!" exclaimed the new boy. "And you were fishing for it in the mud here, young Desnouettes? Off, now! It's easy to see you have forgotten your training, before you are six years out of the streets. Don't you know that sometimes one must fish in the air and hunt in the sea? I'll wager you, now, that thing is right before your eyes, if it is not under your nose; as, for example—" And, with a dash, he plunged into the crowd, whirled about first one and then another, and finally pounced upon an inoffensive-looking old "Bellows-and-buckets-to-mend" man, who, with his basket of bellows strapped on his back, was an idle gazer in the watching crowd.

"So, rascal! You delay the Emperor's message, do you? See, you page, is not this your letter?" and he pulled from beneath the bellows-mender's basket-strap a paper that had been slyly tucked there.

Philip stared in unbelief, and then fell upon his recovered treasure with a shout. Etienne, the equerry, cried in a loud voice: "In the name of the Emperor, seize that man! Police, police!"

But the old bellows-mender protested his innocence in a torrent of denial, and even Philip was compelled to admit the wisdom of his new friend's laughing taunt: "Ho! you page; you will need to go to school to the street again. Don't you know that he who is guilty is not he who is caught? Old bellows-mender could never stick a note under his own strap behind his back, could he, say? Some of our good friends here at hand played that trick on him and you. Having the booty, let the joke pass. The letter is better than the lifter."

"Wise one, let me thank you," Philip said, ready to clasp his benefactor in a warm embrace. "Your name?"

"Then you do not know me?"

"What, I? Why—no!—but so! Why—it is never—"

"Yes?"

"That pig of a Pierre?" Philip blurted out the words in an astonishment of recognition.

"Citizen Pierre Labeau, at your excellency's service," the big boy said, with a mock salute. "Oh, you are not the only one out of our street, Prince Phil, to get your step. Behold me! I am deputy doorkeeper at La Force!"

"The big prison?"

"The same—and where you might have been, young Desnouettes, had I not been clever enough to see through an o'd joke such as our street has ever loved to play upon the high and mighty."

Philip could scarcely speak. Shame and surprise alike filled him with dismay, and almost brought the mist of boyish mortification into his eyes. He had driven through the Street of the Washerwomen just to make "that pig of a Pierre" green with envy; and, behold, Philip was the discomfited one — Pierre, the self-possessed one!

But, quickly, mortification turned to gratitude. He flung out both hands toward his old foeman.

"My friend," he cried, "I owe you much. Where may I see you to-morrow? I am on duty to-day. I wish to — Oh, my head! My heart! I forgot the other!"

"What now?" Pierre inquired, struck by Philip's sudden despair.

"All is ready, Monsieur the Page," Etienne, the equerry, called from the calash.

The finding of the letter had driven the morocco case from Philip's mind, and now the misery broke upon him. The diamond buckle and the morocco case had not been found!

"See, Pierre," he said quickly, and speaking low; "I carried, too, with me a diamond hat-buckle in a brown morocco case. The Empress gave it me last night. That, also, is gone. Miserable me! — what shall I do?"

"Sparklers, eh?" Pierre exclaimed. "That's harder yet. In a brown morocco case? So! Go you about your business. As for me, I will play the detective. Trust to me, and — see, you — hunt me up at La Force to-morrow. Adieu, my prince! My reverence to the Emperor. Tell him I yet look to have Fouché's portfolio as minister of police."

Then he almost forced Philip into the carriage, and, waving him an adieu, led off the crowd in a rousing cheer:

"'MY FRIEND!' PHILIP CRIED, 'I OWE YOU MUCH.'"

"Long live the Emperor! Long live the Emperor's page!"—with what was just then the popular postscript: "Long live the King of Rome!"

To which courtesy—not certain whether it was real or sarcastic—Philip replied with a wave of his befeathered chapeau, and was speedily whirling into the courtyard of the Tuileries.

As he rose to spring from the carriage, his foot struck something small and hard, ambushed beneath the carriage-mat. He pounced upon it at once.

"My faith!" he cried, with gleaming eyes, "the morocco case! Was ever boy luckier than I?"

There it must have fallen in the overturn, and there have lain during all the hunt and worry; and, meantime, Pierre was playing detective for it. Well, he should be enlightened and recompensed next day. Odd that "that pig of a Pierre" should have turned out such a trump, after all.

Thinking these thoughts, Philip entered the palace, a wiser and much more subdued young fellow than had left it in such a blaze of glory only the day before. The boy's pride had suffered sadly, but he had learned a lesson.

Hastily making himself presentable, he delivered to the Emperor the letter from Josephine.

"So; 't is our royal courier. Well done, you page." And taking the letter, he read its words of congratulation and friendship with interest and pleasure. Then he turned to the boy.

"And how looked the Empress?" he asked.

"Well, Sire; and much delighted," Philip replied.

"And did she"—for Napoleon was always inquisitive—"did she remember the messenger?"

"Oh, yes, Sire; royally," the boy made answer.

"So! It was like her. But how?" the Emperor went on.

"With this, Sire." And Philip fished the brown morocco case from the pocket into which he had thrust it.

Napoleon took the case from the boy, and pressed the spring. It flew open, and disclosed to the Emperor— nothing!

Philip gave a start of terror; his legs lost all their stiffness; his eyes grew big with dismay.

"Gone!" he gasped.

"The Empress pays liberally for favors," said Napoleon, grimly; "or else my messengers play the fool with things committed to them. What was in here, boy?"

"A diamond hat-buckle, Sire," the boy replied in a broken and distracted voice.

"And where is it?"

"Alas, Sire!" said Philip, sadly, "I fear it was stolen when the letter was lost."

"The letter? What letter?" cried the Emperor.

The wrath of Napoleon was not a pleasant thing to face. It had withered bigger men than Philip the page. But the boy knew that a straightforward story was his only salvation, and, without flinching, he told the Emperor the whole affair, not even concealing his reasons for driving through the Street of the Washerwomen.

The Emperor listened impassively, and when the end was reached he said: "This, then, is the way you would play the messenger, you boy? You would use the Emperor's time to serve your private ends? Had the letter been lost, your head should have been the forfeit. I confer favors only

"'GONE!' HE GASPED."

where I can trust; I command only those who will obey me. Have I judged wrongly, and may I not trust you, boy? You have betrayed your trust—you, the Courier of the King. Ah, so! I have it! Come with me. The King of Rome, whom you have served so carelessly, shall judge your misdemeanor." And bidding the boy follow him, the Emperor strode on to the imperial nursery.

In his royal cradle lay the royal baby. Napoleon stopped beside the little bed of his son, looked down upon him, and said solemnly:

"Your Majesty, here is your courier. He has been careless in his trust. I present him to you for judgment and sentence. Your Majesty's smile or frown is law. What shall be the verdict? Shall we punish or forgive?"

All this seemed, at first, very absurd to Philip, who had but a boy's contempt for a cradled baby. But he grew serious as the Emperor made his point. He looked down upon the helpless infant, anxiety in his heart, but conciliation in his eye; and as he looked he winked the wink of flattery at the wondering baby.

Thereupon, the royal infant began to "coo" and "goo" with all the gurgle of baby good nature; with wide-open eyes he looked upon the dissembling boy, and, caught by the wink of that designing eye, tossed up one little hand, while the sober baby face broke suddenly into a certain and perceptible smile.

"The King smiles. There you have the verdict, boy," the Emperor said. "His Majesty graciously pardons your misdemeanor, on the condition, if you can translate his sentence, that you never do so again." And Napoleon laughed.

For this singular man had a boy-side to his nature, that spent itself, now and then, in jokes and romps and ear-pulling, not usually associated with an imperial majesty. "Is he not a fine, fat boy, Philip? My head, they say— my eyes. Some day you shall dance 'zig-zag' for him, as you did for that other boy in St. Cloud,—provided you have not, before that time, lost your head through heedlessness, which I fear is not unlikely. But keep your head—we need it for the future. For this young monseigneur here we must build up France; and such as you must help him wear the crown. Go now. You are pardoned. The courier is a page once more. Yes—and see to it that you play detective, too. The diamond buckle must be found. I give you three days and a release from duty to find it. Some day, too, let me see that Pierre boy. He is a shrewd one, and should be good for something. Go; and report the result to me in three days' time."

Philip turned to go; then dropping upon one knee, he kissed, not the Emperor's hand, but—clever boy that he was!—the hand of the baby King. Thereby he won the Emperor's favor anew; for even the great Napoleon was human—and a father!

The next morning, according to agreement, Philip presented himself at the prison of La Force, where were confined those held "under suspicion" of crime or treason. His imperial livery and his page's badge gained him easy entrance, and in response to his inquiry for Pierre, the deputy doorkeeper, that sturdy young fellow was soon hurrying from his post in the Charlemagne Court to greet his visitor.

"So; it is you, Monsieur the Page? See you, now; I have tracked three diamond hat-buckles and two brown morocco cases. Eh? Yes; oh, yes, we can find these things even after they get hidden away in the Court of the Miracles. It is just knowing how to get at them, you see. But when one comes to knowing every thief in the big prisons, as I do, one finds just how to get his information. I have secured some sparklers, I say—perhaps yours, perhaps not. Now what was your buckle like?"

Philip, as well as he could, described the gift of the Empress.

"Yes," Pierre nodded. "I have seen such a one—but not its case."

"That is here," Philip replied. "Behold, then! I found it in the carriage after I left you."

That made the whole matter clear. By cleverly using the knowledge gained by his street education and his prison connection, Pierre had traced out the lost buckle, and Philip was overjoyed.

"To-morrow you shall have it," Pierre promised him. "I can put my hands upon it in an hour when once my lines are set; but not to-day. See now, you Philip! I will deliver the sparklers to you at the Tower of St. Jacques at sunset to-morrow."

"At sunset to-morrow—at the Tower of St. Jacques," Philip repeated. "And meantime, Pierre, my friend" (you see it was no longer "that pig of a Pierre"), "tell me how I can ever repay you for this?"

"Wait until you get your sparklers," replied the deputy doorkeeper of La Force; and then Philip left the great, gloomy prison, that once had been a baron's stronghold, and wandered away to the house in the Street of the Fight. Here he held an audience spell-bound with the story of his travels and his adventures, his mishaps and his experiences, since last they had seen him, and since he had been weighed in the balance and found perhaps just a little wanting as the Courier of the King.

CHAPTER X

THE TOWER OF ST. JACQUES

GRAND and graceful, the Tower of St. Jacques overtopped the tiled roofs of the low buildings and the straggling market that surrounded it. Springing into the air one hundred and seventy-five feet, and surmounted by a delicate spire, the tower stood as at once guide and landmark for all that section of old Paris, from the eastern barriers to the bridges and the palace of the Louvre.

The church of which this stately tower was and is the only survival had been a sanctuary for murderers in the days of the ancient kings, but had itself been pulled down by those later murderers—the rabid revolutionists of the time of the Terror—who could not draw the sharp line that separates liberty from lawlessness.

For so enthusiastic a student of the past as Citizen Daunou the grand old tower had special interest. To this interest had been added the fascinations of relic-hunting; for among the papers that had come under his eye as Keeper of the Archives had been one that spoke of certain valuable relics deposited a generation before in an old crypt beneath the northwestern turret. This crypt, the Keeper of the Archives reasoned, might have escaped the pillage and destruction by the revolutionary mob from the Paris streets; and this he wished to prove to his own satisfaction.

So it happened that on one of the last days of March, in the year 1811, Citizen Daunou was on his way to the Tower of St. Jacques, accompanied by Uncle Fauriel and Mademoiselle. She herself was something of an amateur investigator, and, in her way, quite as interested in the things to be seen and the things to be studied in the quaint sections of old Paris as was the scholarly Keeper himself.

They had left the big Bureau of Archives in the Street of the Wheatfield, and with all the ingenuity and assurance of the born Parisian had threaded their way through the network of narrow streets which separated the bureau from the tower; for in the opening years of the nineteenth century it was no easy task for any one but a born Parisian to pick a secure way through the great city's narrow and tortuous streets.

They had skipped the flowing gutters, jumped the piles of rubbish, cleared the thousand and one impediments, dodged the ceaseless, pushing throng of peddlers, pedestrians, carriers, and cartmen, on both roadway and sidewalk, until panting Uncle Fauriel, pausing for breath in the doorway of a convenient wine-shop in the Street of the Fox, had mopped his perspiring head and puffed out: "It may be all well enough for you two—one long and lean, and the other young and frisky—to rush along at this rate, but I am getting too fat for your fun. I've dodged every cart and every carrier in Paris; I've jumped the gutters and pulled myself in like a Gascon. Time was when I could do it as well as you, and travel the streets without getting a speck of dust or a spot of mud, as spick and span as Mademoiselle here; but it's gone by—it's gone by. I'm too fat for the narrow streets, and too clumsy for the muddy ones. Go slower, or get me a cab."

But Mademoiselle did not hear his complainings. She was conscious only of certain words her quick ears had caught from amid the passing crowd:

"One of Nicholas's boys, he is; name of Desnouettes. It's to be a big haul, eh? Sunset—Tower of St. Jacques; and he says—"

This was all she heard; the voices were lost in the crowd. She had not even caught sight of the speaker; but it was quite enough for Mademoiselle. Some danger threatened Philip; for he was Desnouettes. He was one of "Nicholas's boys"—the nickname by which the streets of Paris recognized Napoleon's pages.

She thought quickly. Could she warn Philip? She did not know where to find him; for he had told her he was to be "off duty" as a page that day. Should she tell her father? No, he would laugh at her; so, too, would Uncle Fauriel. They would "pooh-pooh" the idea of danger; they would tell her that Philip was big enough to take care of himself, and that it was no matter for maids to meddle with.

And yet that voice in the crowd might mean danger to Philip. He had not told her of his rendezvous at the Tower of St. Jacques; he had told her merely that Pierre had promised to restore the Empress's gift that day. Perhaps it was a trap. What ought she to do?—what could she do?

A brilliant plan flashed upon her. The Emperor! He could do anything. Why, then, should he not protect his pages? And Philip was his favorite.

Her mind was quickly made up.

"Papa, I am going back," she declared. "Go you with Uncle Fauriel, and go slowly; for he *is* such a hot old dear just now. Perhaps I should only be in the way if you are to climb and poke about in the old tower. I have just thought of something I must do. Never mind me; I can get back all right."

And even while the two relic-hunters looked at her, puzzled over a girl's fickleness, she was off with a wave of the hand before they could make a protest, and, hurrying across to the historic Street of St. Honoré, was soon speeding away to the Tuileries.

She ran along the terrace to the Floral Gate. To the grenadier on guard outside she preferred her request.

"The Emperor, Mademoiselle? Have you, then, an admittance order?"

"Alas, no. I must see him on urgent affairs — a matter of life and death," the girl said breathlessly.

"So; is it as bad as that?" the guard queried. "I will summon my corporal — or, see! my faith, Mademoiselle! you are in luck, you. Look! there is the Emperor himself."

Out of the doorway that led to the private apartments of the Emperor in the Floral Pavilion of the great palace came a short, stout man in a green overcoat. Mademoiselle knew him at once. It was her friend of the Boulogne woods; it was the Emperor.

A light carriage surrounded by a small cavalry escort of guardsmen stood in the inner court. The big doors of the Floral Gate were wide open.

"Run, Mademoiselle, now," the guardsman whispered.

"'SAVE HIM, SIRE!' SHE EXCLAIMED."

"It is your only chance! You must not lose it. As for me—I see nothing." And, with that, he turned away.

Almost before the words were said, the girl had scurried through the open gateway. Keyed up to the demand laid upon her, she was thoughtless of everything save her desire to be in time to rescue Philip from danger.

The Emperor's foot was on the carriage-step. Straight toward the carriage rushed the girl, her hands stretched out to the little man in a green coat.

"Save him, Sire!" she exclaimed.

Ushers and officers looked down at the girl, startled and shocked by this breach of stiff court etiquette; and even the statue-like guardsmen almost moved. The Emperor, still with his foot on the wide carriage-step, turned in surprise; for he had peculiar views as to the proper "sphere" of women and girls, and this sudden assault quite staggered him.

"Well, well, sirs," he said, "what have we here? Who is the girl? Save whom—save whom, child?"

"Philip, Sire; your page—page Desnouettes!" she cried. "He is in danger—danger of his life!"

"Page Desnou—ah! our detective, eh? And you are—?"

"I? Why, I am Lucie Dannou, Sire."

"Dannou? Dannou?" the Emperor mused. "What—the Keeper of the Archives? And you are the citizen's daughter, and young Desnouettes's friend? Well, then, what of this danger? What is it? Here, sit you by me, and tell the doleful tale." And he handed the young petitioner to one of the small and stiff but gilded settees that stood in the Floral Pavilion. "Oh, sit, child! Never mind ceremony;

this is not a public reception." And he made her sit at his side. Then she told her story.

"Not much to go by, that," the Emperor remarked, as Mademoiselle reached the end. "And yet it may mean mischief. Philip was to receive back the lost hat-buckle to-day, was he? He has tracked it well. We must not let the chance of losing it again come to him. But how could those rascals know it? Is that Pierre boy playing him false? At the Tower of St. Jacques, you say. We will set a watch. Ho, Meneval! See that we drive first to Baron Pasquier's at the Ministry of Police. Never fear, child; Philip shall come to no such harm. There, run along; or—wait—you must be tired. Come, you shall see the baby."

"Oh, Sire! The King of Rome?" The girl clapped her hands for joy.

"The baby, the baby, child!" And then this ruler of kings caught the girl by the hand, and together—"Just as if he might have been Uncle Fauriel," Mademoiselle afterward said—they hurried along the corridor and into the royal nursery. For, despite his imperial aims and his conquering schemes, no man, when he desired, was more "one of the people" than was the First Napoleon. And on the subject of "that baby" he was as proud a father as ever breathed.

Mademoiselle looked and worshiped to her heart's content, and quite captured the Emperor's heart by her loyal enthusiasm.

Seeing that the young girl glanced from the baby's face to his own, the Emperor smiled, saying: "He looks like me,—this baby here?"

"THEN SHE TOLD HER STORY."

"Oh, so much, Sire!" Mademoiselle replied.

"Of course he does," the Emperor assented. "We all say so here; is it not so, Madame?" he added, turning to the baby's governess, Madame de Montesquiou. Then to Mademoiselle: "Why, he is as much like me as—why, as you are like Philip."

"I like Philip, Sire?" the girl exclaimed.

"To be sure," replied the Emperor, taking Mademoiselle's chin between his fingers and scanning her pretty face. "You should be his sister, one would say."

"But how could that be, Sire?" said the girl. "He is Desnouettes."

"And you are Daunou. *Are* you Daunou, child?" the Emperor said, with a searching look at Mademoiselle.

"Why, of course, Sire; who else should I be?" the girl rejoined.

"Of course, who else?" the Emperor echoed; then he added musingly, "I have known Citizen Daunou—let me see—ever since the days of the Directory; and I never heard of the Citizeness Daunou. Do you remember your mother, child?"

"Why, no, Sire; she died when I was but a baby like his Majesty here," Mademoiselle replied.

"Ah, yes; to be sure, like his Majesty here. And now must we take leave of his Majesty here, and think of a bigger boy. For our knight is in danger, and he must be succored. But see you, pretty one," the Emperor said, again taking Mademoiselle's chin between his fingers and looking in her eyes, "I have a message for you: My compliments to Citizen Daunou, and tell him that, like all old republicans, he is but an owl when the sunlight comes, and cannot see beyond his spectacles. Just tell him that for me, will you, child?"

And dropping the girl's chin, the Emperor pinched her ear till she "ouched!" in spite of herself, whereupon the Emperor laughed merrily, and even the King in the cradle gurgled in fun.

"I will tell him so, Sire," Mademoiselle replied dutifully, "since you command it. But—is it respectful for me thus to speak to my father?"

"When the Emperor uses you as a mouthpiece, girl, anything is respectful," was the Emperor's decision. "And now, kiss his Majesty's hand. The audience is over."

Mademoiselle dropped prettily on one knee beside the golden cradle, and kissed the dimpled little hand that the nurse uncovered for her. Then a page conducted her to the outer gate, but not before she had received the Emperor's parting word: "I will see to Philip's safety, little one. And do you remember my message to Citizen Daunou: an owl in the sunlight, eh?"

And in the royal nursery Madame de Montesquiou, the little King's governess, said: "Well, nurse, if the Emperor is to bring all the children in Paris to see the little King, we might as well be in the House of St. Vincent de Paul as in the imperial palace. We shall have his little Majesty catching some disease yet, with all this hand-kissing." But, then, Madame de Montesquiou was very jealous of her royal little charge, and, if possible, would have kept him under a glass case.

The Emperor did not forget his promise to Mademoiselle. That very afternoon, fully an hour before sunset, the Tower of St. Jacques was put under watch by detectives, while in the market at its foot a detachment of armed police held themselves in readiness to answer a call for help. The market was searched, the surrounding space was watched, even the old tower itself was twice hunted through for suspicious characters. But no Pierre, no Philip, and no ambushed kidnappers were to be seen or "spotted."

What could it mean? Had Mademoiselle's ears deceived her? Had she "fooled" the Emperor?

And, meantime, where was Philip?

CHAPTER XI

THE PUPILS OF THE GUARD

THE Emperor had been "fooled." For even while detectives and policemen were searching the old Tower of St. Jacques, Philip the page, who had never been near it at all, was walking calmly toward the Street of the Fight, with the recovered hat-buckle safe in his pocket, and in his mind an ardent desire somehow to repay Pierre.

He had haunted the crooked streets of the dirty quarter in which he had come so signally to grief, hoping to gain some clue that would put him on the track of the marauders. When a boy's pride is hurt he will not rest until he can regain his self-esteem, and Philip felt that his duty lay in bringing the guilty ones to justice. If he could do this without the help of Pierre, the deputy doorkeeper, it would prove that boys could be just as wide-awake in the Tuileries as among the strange things that went on at La Force.

So, no longer in his imperial livery of crimson and gold, but in the every-day dress of a Paris boy, Philip was seeking to put to good use his old education of the street, when suddenly, in the narrow and dirty Street of Jean Lantier, near to the unsavory Court of the Miracles, he ran plump against Pierre.

The amateur detectives looked keenly at each other. Then

the boy from La Force said to the boy from the Tuileries:
"What, it is you, young Desnouettes? And doing what?"

"Hunting those fellows down, my Pierre," Philip replied. "I don't like to let things go unsettled."

"And could you not trust me, Monsieur the Page? You gain nothing by pushing things."

"I can gain my lost standing at the palace," Philip responded.

"But leave it to me, my boy," said Pierre. "Such a hunt is more in my line than in yours. And we are both ahead of time, we two; but I have your sparklers."

"Good boy, Pierre!" cried jubilant Philip; and added, with boyish assurance, "the Emperor will repay you. Give me the buckle."

"But not in the street, stupid! Would you lose it again?" the young detective whispered. "Come you with me—say to Citizen Popon's. You remember the place?"

Remember it? Did he not, though? It was the dark wine-cellar in which Philip had overheard the plot against the Emperor, and from which he reckoned the days of his good fortune.

So it came to pass that in the dingy wine-cellar of Citizen Popon, rather than at the old Tower of St. Jacques, the page recovered his lost treasure, and said again and again: "My faith! but you are a clever one—you Pierre. However can I repay you?"

"Wait until I ask you for payment, my Philip," was Pierre's reply; and then and there this successful young amateur detective flatly refused any compensation for tracking the lost gift of an empress. In so doing lay his shrewdness; for Pierre, though a good fellow, was always looking out for Number One. "Philip is a page of the palace, a favorite of the Emperor, and bound to rise," he reasoned. "If he owes me return for a favor he will always bear me in mind, and I may gain a new step by not taking from him now. It is better to be generous than greedy, and in the end it pays better."

Thus sharply he reasoned; but he simply said, "It's for old friendship's sake, my boy." And so, after a long talk, the boys separated. Pierre went back to his post at the prison of La Force; Philip, hugging close his rescued treasure, sought, not the imperial palace, but the house in the quiet Street of the Fight. There Mademoiselle met him.

"Oh, Philip!" she cried. "And it is you? Tell me quickly! What happened? How did they save you?"

"What happened?" Philip queried. "'Save' me? Where?"

"Why, at the Tower of St. Jacques," Mademoiselle replied impatiently. "I found it all out. What happened?"

"But I do not understand you, Mademoiselle," said puzzled Philip. "I have not been to the Tower of St. Jacques."

"No?" Mademoiselle cried excitedly. "And you were not set upon by brigands?"

"Why, no," said the boy. "You see, I met Pierre in the Street of Jean Lantier, before I had reached the tower. And see, here is the buckle. I have it safe once more."

"But, mercy! what must the Emperor think?" Mademoiselle almost wailed, scarce noticing the brilliants that had made all the bother. "He will say I misled him.

PHILIP'S GRATITUDE.

Dear me, dear me! Now it is I that am in the wrong, and who will right me?"

Much perplexed, Philip asked for an explanation, and

Mademoiselle told her story, and how she had petitioned the Emperor.

"But you saved my life, Mademoiselle," exclaimed the grateful Philip, "even if the danger did not come to me. For, had I not met Pierre before the time appointed, I should have been at the Tower at sunset. Mademoiselle, I thank you"; and, true to the courtliness which had become a part of his daily training, Philip bent over the girl's hand, and kissed it in knightly fashion.

"It is not for me to remain here," he said. "I must hasten to the palace and explain it all. Trust me, Mademoiselle; I will set you right with the Emperor."

Then Citizen Daunou, who had entered the room while Mademoiselle was telling her story, said: "I may be an owl, Mademoiselle, though why the Emperor should say so passes my knowledge. But this explains certain things. Uncle Fauriel and I lingered late over our researches in the tower; and—would you believe it?—Uncle Fauriel was very nearly arrested by two officials from the Ministry of Police. Uncle Fauriel is so rabid a republican, you know, that he is ever under suspicion; and but for my being recognized by the sergeant of police who came from the market with his men, we should, I think, have been compelled to accompany the detectives as suspicious persons. My faith, though! Is not that the rarest joke? Uncle Fauriel and I were, I now see, very nearly under arrest as the intending assassins of my friend Monsieur the Page, under the special protection of the Emperor. Away, Sir Page! It is not safe for you to linger here. Behold your assassin!"

And Citizen Daunou laughed so heartily that even Mademoiselle's perplexed face broke into smiles, and Philip appreciated the joke quite as fully. But, all the same, it did not free him from a little trepidation as, on his way back to the palace, he thought over the affairs of the day, and prepared himself for a scene with the Emperor.

The "scene," however, was but a mild one. Napoleon had far more important things on his mind than the trials of pages and the woes of over-zealous maidens. Philip, too, had the advantage of being first on the ground. He had made his explanations before the report came from the police; and the Emperor, being spared the confusion that this report might otherwise have created, held the key to the situation, and, happily, looked on it all as a good joke.

"But you were never cut out for a detective, young Desnouettes," he said. "Leave that to others, and do, rather, the duties that are nearest you. As for the girl, she is a bright little creature and a wise one. She meant well. It was only you that blundered into safety without knowing, and so spoiled her excellent little drama. That boy Pierre seems to have been the cleverest one of the lot. I must— see here, you boy; do you know anything of your father?"

Startled at this sudden change of subject, Philip looked surprised, but said, "Nothing more than you do, Sire. I have told you all I know of him."

"Nor of your family?"

"Nothing, Sire."

"So! Well—let me see that Pierre boy; some day I may find use for his cleverness."

And Philip was dismissed, relieved but puzzled.

But so many other things were afoot in that busy summer of 1811 that a boy's concerns were speedily forgotten, and even the boy himself was so full of crowding duties as to have little time for queries and conjectures.

The month of June was one round of festivity, ceremonial, and display. It was the baptismal month of the baby King of Rome.

Napoleon the Emperor was at the height of his power. Kings were his vassals, and conquered nations were his domains. All of Europe, save only Russia and the British Isles, was subject or ally to France. The little man in the green uniform was the foremost man of all the world.

He had won his eminence by the force of his genius, the strength of his will, the brilliancy of his successes, and by hard work. For in all his vast domain there was no more tireless worker than the Emperor Napoleon the First.

No one appreciated this more than Philip the page. Many a time, far into the night, had he waited the imperial commands, or run upon the imperial errands, until tired legs refused to do their duty, and the curly head dropped, dead with sleep, upon the wearied arm.

The month of June in the year 1811 seemed the crowning point of all the magnificence of the First Empire. It was a month of display—one continued fête—in honor of the little King's baptism.

Philip had been one of the retinue that had escorted the imperial family from St. Cloud to the Tuileries on the afternoon of the sixth of June. With the other pages he had hung upon the backboard of the imperial coach, as on the next day—Sunday, the seventh of June—it was driven through a living lane of glittering helmets and nodding

plumes, where a double row of the troops of the line and of
the Imperial Guard stretched from the palace of the Tuileries
to the cathedral of Notre Dame. Under the garlanded
portal and into the brilliantly lighted church he had passed
as one of the glittering procession. Within, as one amid that
notable throng of princes and peers, of great officials of the
crown, of cardinals and bishops and archbishops, of the senate, the court, and the mayors of the great cities of the Empire, Philip had "assisted" at the ceremony. It was a sight
never to be forgotten, when, regal in a coat of silver tissue
embroidered with ermine; with his train upheld by a marshal of the Empire; with his mother, the Empress, walking
in imperial state under one gorgeous canopy, and his famous
father, the Emperor, under another gorgeous canopy; with
a princess bearing his baptismal candle, a princess holding
his chrism-cloth, a countess carrying his salt-cellar, and all
about him princes and dukes, chamberlains and marshals,
grand "eagles," grand equerries, grand masters, and grand—
lots of other things; with ushers and heralds and orderlies
and pages; supported by his nurses and governesses; with
an emperor for a godfather and a queen for a godmother—
this one little baby, Francis Charles Joseph Napoleon Bonaparte, King of Rome and heir to France, was presented for
baptism at the high altar of the grand old church which had
been the scene of so many great and marvelous and curious
ceremonials, but never of one more magnificent than this.

So the baby was baptized. Then, in sight of the whole
assembly, while the organ pealed out the "Jubilate," and the
First Herald at Arms, standing in the choir, cried out,
"Long live the King of Rome!" the baby's proud father

held his son aloft where all might see His Little Magnificence. Then all the crowded church, all the packed square without, and all the listening city raised a mighty shout: "Long live the King of Rome! Long live the Emperor!"

Do you imagine that Philip would have missed that? Not for the world! His voice was hoarse from shouting; his face was flushed with enthusiasm. He was proud of his position; proud that he was alive; proud that he was a Frenchman, that he was a boy of Paris, that he was a page of the Emperor!

Nor would he willingly have missed the great entertainment at the City Hall, where, after the baptismal ceremony, the Emperor dined in public, with his crown upon his head, the Empress by his side, kings and queens on his right and left, for all the world like that great Emperor of old,—Charlemagne,—whose state he patterned after, and whose title he assumed. For, you see, the Emperor Napoleon was always dramatic, always startling, always effective, in whatever he undertook. Whether he kidnapped a king, or stole a pope, or "absorbed" a kingdom, or won a battle, or gave a ball, he did it so splendidly that even his enemies marveled, and all the world wondered at the audacity of this little man who had carved his way from nothing to a throne, and had filled the world with his name.

To this baptismal ceremony and banquet succeeded days and days of magnificence. And Philip was able to make the claim of the old Roman: "All of which I saw, and part of which I was." For, as the page of the palace, he was on duty at almost every "high function."

There were banquets and balls, shows and processions,

NAPOLEON REVIEWS THE PUPILS OF THE GUARD.

festivals and fêtes, street parades and water parades, tournaments, fireworks, and balloon ascensions, and everything that busy brains could devise or lavish expenditure could procure to please the people, show the grandeur of the Empire, and do honor to the one who, probably, took the least interest in it all—a pretty little baby boy, only three months old.

At the Tuileries, at St. Cloud, at stately Versailles, and at beautiful Rambouillet, the summer passed in pleasure and parade and blaze of glory; for these were the palmy days of the Empire, the climax of Napoleon's power.

And one day in the Place of the Carrousel, the great open square in front of the palace of the Tuileries, where the Emperor held his weekly reviews of the Imperial Guard, there came a new surprise.

It was a beautiful August day. The splendid palace, outlined against the clear Parisian sky, made a grand background for the mass of moving color, as battalion after battalion wheeled and circled and charged and manœuvered. Cavalry and infantry marched and countermarched, plumes nodded, bayonets flashed, helmets glittered, bands played, display was everywhere.

Then, while the regiments stood at rest, the gay strains of other military bands were heard, and into the square, beneath the triumphal arch crowned by the great bronze horses of St. Mark's (which "the conqueror" had brought from Venice), there came, rank upon rank, in soldierly array, spick and span in their new uniforms of green and gold, eight thousand little foot-soldiers, not one of whom was yet in his teens.

As steadily as veterans, as solid as the Old Guard itself,

every boy doing his best, every eye "front," every hand shouldering a toy musket or carrying a dwarf sword, the Lilliputian battalions halted and faced the smiling veterans.

The Emperor appeared. The boys went through their manœuvers with precision and ease. And when the review was over the Emperor, standing midway between his veterans and his boy brigade, pointed to the little soldiers, and said to his grenadiers:

"Soldiers of my Guard, behold your children! These are the Pupils of the Guard, the sons of those who have fallen in battle for France, the defenders upon whose valor the future of my empire must rest. To them I confide the guarding of my son, as I have confided myself to you. For them I require, from you, friendship and protection."

Then facing the boyish brigade, he said: "My children, in attaching you to my Guard I give you a difficult duty. But I shall trust in you. I know that some day it will be said of you: 'These children are worthy of their fathers.' Pupils of the Guard! from this day you are in the service of the King of Rome."

"Long live the Emperor!" From the Guard and its " Pupils," and from the thousands who witnessed the double review, the mighty shout went up. Philip's voice helped to swell the shout. He had regarded the little Pupils of the Guard with all that patronage of superiority that fifteen accords to ten. But he was enthusiastic none the less, and led off in a fresh hail of "Long live the King of Rome! Long live the Pupils of the Guard!"

In the midst of this outburst his shout changed suddenly to a cry of recognition and joy. For, in the little knot of non-commissioned officers who had accompanied the Pupils of the Guard, and whom he supposed to be their preceptors, he caught a glimpse of a familiar face. That wooden leg, that grizzled mustache, that stalwart figure, that proudly displayed cross of the Legion of Honor, that air of confidence and self-recognized ability—it could be none other! In a moment Philip had rushed across the parade, and flung himself upon the unresisting veteran.

The boy's eyes had not played him false. It was old Corporal Peyrolles—Peyrolles the wooden-legged—Peyrolles of St. Cyr!

CHAPTER XII

HOW PHILIP BAITED THE RUSSIAN BEAR

PEYROLLES! Dear old Peyrolles! Where, then, do you come from?" Philip cried, hugging the veteran in a frenzy of delight.

"Why, your Serene Mightiness, if your Imperial Magnificence will but grant me space to breathe," Corporal Peyrolles replied, struggling to salute his captor, "I would say in answer, from the School of the Pupils of the Guard at Vincennes, most Noble Nobility."

"And when did you leave St. Cyr?"

"With your Excellency's permission, I would answer, your Serene Mightiness, just two months ago."

"But whatever is the matter with you, 'high-mightinessing' me like that, you Peyrolles?" Philip cried, casting a laughing look of puzzled inquiry upon the veteran's stolid face. "Why—don't you know me?—me—Cadet Desnouettes of St. Cyr?"

"So! Is it young Desnouettes?" exclaimed Peyrolles, catching the boy by the arm. "Why, to be sure—the very same boy—or, pardon me—your Imperial Excellency. And what may you be, all so fine in your crimson and gold?"

"Why, what should I be?" Philip replied. "A page of the palace, of course."

"What! over a year at court, and only a page yet?" Peyrolles exclaimed. "You are slow, you boy. By this time, as titles are going yonder, you should be a Hereditary Grand Duke, or a First Grand Marshal of the Blood Royal, at the very least."

"You dear old grumbler!" cried Philip, giving the veteran another hug. And then he laughed; for now he saw through Peyrolles's perplexing play with imperial adjectives. The old fellow did not approve of this flow of titles and honors that pervaded the court of the Emperor. Corporal Peyrolles was jealous.

"Why, look you, young Desnouettes," he said; "you can't throw a stone in Paris, anywhere, without hitting a title. And what were they all? No better than Peyrolles once. Murat a king! I marched with him at Arcola. Ney a prince! I fought beside him at Marengo. Bessières a duke! I saved his life at Austerlitz. Duroc a grand something or other at the palace! I helped him through the sand at the Pyramids. Why, even old Limpfoot, Talleyrand, whom we drove out of the republic for an emigrant, is a prince, if you please, and weaves his web about the Emperor."

The old corporal grew so heated over this title-giving to those whom he had known as "nobodies" and subalterns, that Philip was forced to stop the tirade for fear of listeners.

But Peyrolles was right, none the less. The craze for titles and position was undermining the Empire. The Corsican lieutenant who had been the friend of the Robespierres, the general of the Revolution who had made the Republic triumphant over the kings of Europe, had now become as great a royalist as Louis XVI., as firm an upholder of the divine right of kings as his father-in-law, the Emperor of Austria. He was welcoming back the emigrant nobles who had been exiled because they were royalists, and was scattering titles among his supporters like prizes at a rifle-match.

But though an old soldier of the Republic like Peyrolles might grumble, and an old revolutionist like Uncle Fauriel might growl, the attaché of an imperial court like Philip,— a boy who adored his Emperor, and had place and perquisites at the court,— could look neither beneath nor beyond the daily life of which he was a part. "Who knows?" he said: "I may be a prince some day. There is a chance for every boy now, in France." An ambitious lad, even if he did stop to think of things, would be a believer in honors and titles and rewards of merit.

But Philip was delighted to be so near his dear old Peyrolles once more, and they talked of old times until the call to duty drew the veteran to his barracks and the page to his palace.

This very day of the review of the Pupils of the Guard, there was a grand reception at the Tuileries. The Emperor received.

The splendid palace was thronged with guests—representatives of every nation in Europe—vassal kings, allied princes, titled ambassadors, peers and marshals of France, high officials, famous citizens, dashing soldiers, grand ladies, ushers and pages.

Among the pages was Philip. With a half-dozen of his

brothers in livery, he stood by the big door that opened into the splendid Hall of the Marshals. Here they awaited the arrival of the Emperor, who was making a tour of the palace and greeting or conversing with the great ones who were present at the reception.

The pages, boy-like, were discussing everything—criticizing this person, making fun of that, and getting food for talk in whatever came uppermost, from the toilets of the ladies and the awkwardness of the "provincials" to the last hotly contested game of "bars," the greased-pole climbing at the public sports in the Field of Mars, and the foreign policy of the Emperor; for in all ages boys have been the same— making "talk" out of everything.

In all such boy-talks Philip always stood as the champion of the Emperor. He was at once apologist and applauder; but, with him, approval was real. Boys who have faith in their heroes are the most uncompromising of partizans. Whether Napoleon trod on the toes of Prussia, or snapped his fingers in the face of England, Philip was ready to approve without thinking why, and to shout: "Serves 'em right! Long live the Emperor!"

Especially was this true of our page when, cautiously, systematically, and determinedly, the Emperor of the French began to prepare the field for a great hunting of the Russian Bear. And, on the day of the reception, talk of this now historic hunt was rife at Paris; for the relations between Emperor and Czar were daily growing more and more strained.

So, as the pages grouped themselves about the doorway of the great Hall of the Marshals, the conversation gradually drifted toward the subject that was uppermost, whereupon one of the boys boldly declared that when England was whipped out of Spain,—as of course England would be,—that would end the war. For Prince Talleyrand, he said, wanted peace.

"Pouf! Old Limpfoot! What has he got to say about it?" Philip exclaimed indignantly.

"Careful, young Desnouettes," one of the pages whispered, with a not very gentle nudge. "Limpfoot's around somewhere. Not so loud, you, or your ears may smart."

"Well, it makes me mad, that!" Philip declared, but with lowered voice. "Much Talleyrand knows about it! He got his discharge long ago. He's nothing to say. The Emperor, he's the one to decide; and the Emperor, I tell you, is bound to take it out of Russia. The Czar has been wild ever since he had to give in that day on the raft at Tilsit."

"That may be," the peace page rejoined; "but he's not mad enough to fight. If he were, he would have pitched into us when the Emperor said 'No, thank you,' at the time Russia offered him the princess for a wife. The Czar won't fight. Catch-a-Sneezy said so."

"Ah! did he? And what does Catch-a-Sneezy know about it?" Philip exclaimed, a bit contemptuously. "He is but a spy, anyhow."

"No, sir; he is a fine man, Catch-a-Sneezy is," declared Victor. "He gave me two napoleons for slipping him into the Emperor's study one day."

"Yes; to listen and to spy," Philip retorted, so forgetful as to raise his voice again. "I am surprised at you, you Victor. I tell you, Catch-a-Sneezy was a spy."

"And who, now, might this Catch-a-Sneezy be, young sir?"

The query came from a big, bejeweled man close at Philip's elbow. The pages caught their breath, and nudged each other excitedly. "Young Desnouettes has got himself into a pretty mess," they whispered. The questioner was Prince Kourakin, the Russian ambassador.

Philip looked around, a trifle dismayed. But, with true boyish heedlessness, he went on: "Why—that's what we call Monsieur de Sneezy—Zernzy—Czernicheff, your highness," Philip explained, struggling with the unpronounceable name of the Russian who, it was claimed, had played the spy in Paris.

"And you dare to call the aide-de-camp of the Czar a spy, you boy!" the Ambassador said indignantly. "Have a care; have a care, young sir! Such a word spoken at the court of the Czar would cost even you—boy though you are—your liberty, and cause you to feel the whip."

"But this is France, and not Russia, your highness," Philip replied with spirit. "Our Emperor does not knout his boys as Old Alec does."

"Old Alec? Rascally one! But this passes a jest," cried the angry Ambassador. "Be careful, young Insolence! You speak of the Czar of all the Russias. He is too great a man for a graceless boy like you to nickname thus."

"What if he is?" cried heedless Philip, while the other pages felt alternate pride and terror at the audacity of their colleague. "Great as he is, our Little Corporal could eat him at a mouthful."

The quick temper of the Russian, irritated at the thought

of being thus badgered by a boy, and for the instant forgetful of his dignity and surroundings,—stirred, too, by other things that had come to his ears that day,—flamed up at this boyish impudence. The words had scarce passed the page's lips when the hand of the Ambassador flew out, and a sudden and stinging cuff fell upon the boy's ear.

Then Philip lost his temper. He even forgot for an instant to be a gentleman—the thing upon which he most prided himself.

"Ah, Cossack!" he cried. "But that is like you Russians—to strike at those not your size. This is not Poland, sir; this is France. And you, Monsieur the Ambassador—you are a coward!"

The pages stood ready to back up their comrade, and in a ring about the minister glared at him like angry dogs holding a bear at bay. But the Ambassador had recovered himself, and with a scornful laugh turned on his heel and walked away to join his brother ambassadors. At that instant the voice of the usher announced, "The Emperor!"—and there, in the doorway, while the pages lined up on both sides to honor the entrance of their master, stood the little man in the chasseur's uniform—the Emperor Napoleon. Philip hoped his indiscretion had escaped the imperial eye; for few indeed, save those concerned in it, had noticed the serio-comic drama. With an ear yet tingling, and a face yet hot with the flush of anger, but feeling, nevertheless, that he had the best of the encounter, Philip bowed low among the other pages as the Emperor passed between them.

And Victor whispered, "My faith! but that was a narrow escape for you, my Philip. I only wish it were over.

PHILIP AND THE RUSSIAN AMBASSADOR.

You 'll catch it yet, I fear. The bear is sharpening his teeth for you; and he bites. If he growls at the Emperor, though—whoop!"

He must have growled a bit; for ere long the boys heard, as did every one else in the room, the voice of Napoleon rising loud and cuttingly, while the Russian statesman, concealing his discomfiture under a smile, took the scolding with scarce a word of protest.

That scolding is now historic. It grew into a harangue, and for full ten minutes it continued unchecked. Philip indeed had baited the Russian Bear, and now Sir Bruin stood at bay before the chief of the pack. Over his back Napoleon barked at Russia and snapped at the Czar. "Choose," he said, "between the English and me. I alone can help you. If you threaten, I can fight; and where then will you be? You Russians are like a hare shot in the back: it gets up on its hind legs to look around, and ouf! another shot takes the fool in its head." And so on, and so on, while Philip hugged himself with glee, and the other pages looked and listened with astonishment.

Prince Kourakin, when the Emperor's breath had spent itself in words, withdrew in haste.

"I am suffocated!" Philip heard the Russian declare to his colleague the Ambassador of Prussia. "I must get into the air. It is very hot in the audience-room of the Emperor."

As he passed he glared at Philip, and the page, true to the boy-love for teasing, could not restrain a passing shot. "It is not Poland, it is France, your highness," he said. "But, now—who gets the knout?"

The next instant, however, he regretted his hasty speech. He knew he had violated all the proprieties of court etiquette and dignity. And this, he was well aware, the Emperor never overlooked.

A hand fell upon his shoulder, and he recognized the voice of Malvirade, the First Page.

"To the Emperor, young Desnouettes. He calls you. Come—quickly, quickly; he is in haste."

And Philip, bracing himself for a "scene," faced about and went boldly forward "to take his medicine like a little man." For Philip, though heedless often, was never a coward.

CHAPTER XIII

WHAT MADEMOISELLE FOUND IN THE STREET OF ST. ANTHONY

THE great Hall of the Marshals had almost emptied itself of guests as the Emperor had scored the Ambassador. When big nations quarrel, little states stand from under. After such a bout as was this, when France taunted Russia, none knew upon whom the imperial bolt might fall next; and both vassals and allies had business elsewhere.

Men whispered to one another: "It means war. Thus did the Emperor break out against Whitworth, the Englishman, before the war that ended in the subjugation of Germany; thus did he score Metternich, the Austrian, before the campaign that ended in victory at Wagram. It is peace no longer."

But Philip thought not of the quarrels of states, as he stood before the Emperor. He knew he had been indiscreet. He expected what English boys call a "wigging," and what American boys know as a "hauling over the coals."

"So, young Desnouettes," the Emperor broke out, "you forget yourself in the presence of my guests; is it not so? You dare to bandy words with the representative of a nation, do you? Feather-head! Can I, then, not trust my pages to learn manners?"

"Sire, the Russian angered me, and—I forgot myself," the boy confessed.

"And does that make matters right?" cried Napoleon. "Courtesy should never forget itself."

Then Philip looked squarely into the imperial eye. "Sire," he said, "I did but follow my Emperor."

At this bold declaration every listener looked aghast. Courtiers knew not whether to smile or to frown. Pages held their breath. Only Victor, the irrepressible, whispered:

"My faith! there goes boy Philip's head."

But one never knew how to take that curious compound of severity and sentiment—Napoleon the Emperor. At Philip's words a gleam of anger filled his eye; then, suddenly and strangely, it changed to a twinkle. He tweaked the page's ear—that ear still smarting from the Russian cuff.

"Monkey!" he said. "One might say the Emperor did but follow the page. What caused it all?"

"I said, Sire," Philip replied, "that Catch-a—that Monsieur de Czernicheff was a spy."

"My faith, boy, you spoke the truth. I tell you, gentlemen, the lad spoke the truth," Napoleon cried, turning to his courtiers, who now saw that it was policy to smile, and to cultivate this plucky young page. "That silken Cossack was a spy, and none of you dared tell him so. But you did wrong, you page, to meddle thus with what is not your concern. You are too honest, I fear, to succeed at court. You will be forever in the water that is hot. We must use you elsewhere. Report in the morning at my study. I will devise some return for your over-zeal. Go!"

And Philip went.

In the Blue Room he ran against Citizen Daunou.

"What is this I hear, my son?" that good man said, drawing the page into a deserted corner. "You have been baiting the Russian bear, have you? Tell me of it."

Philip told his story.

"So! see what hot fires we kindle at the court," Citizen Daunou said. "A bad air, a bad air, I fear. When boys bluster, old men hold their peace. And what is to come of it all?"

"That I do not know, Citizen," the page replied. "The Emperor is to render judgment in the morning."

"And our Philip will be a victim or a marshal before another sunset," Citizen Daunou declared. "Well, if the one, you have a friend in me, my boy; if the other—pray let me have a friend in you, Monsieur the Marshal! One never can count on the Emperor. He is full of surprises. But, Philip, this means war. We must face the bear at bay; and what France needs now is peace."

"But the glory of it, Citizen Daunou! There is no glory in peace," cried warlike Philip.

"My son," said the old republican solemnly, "peace hath the greater victories—nay, peace is the greatest of all victories. He who holds back the sword when it is in his power to strike is the hero, the victor, the conqueror, whom time will applaud, and posterity praise. Remember this. Oh, that the Emperor might feel it! Oh, that France might make test of it! But the blood-madness is upon us, and the Empire is doomed."

Philip pondered long—for a boy—over these solemn words of Citizen Daunou. But he dismissed them finally as the theories of one who had no love for the Emperor's methods, and he felt glad that none but himself had heard the remarks. For just then it was scarcely wise to talk peace in the imperial palace, whose indomitable master desired a new war of conquest.

Next morning Philip obeyed orders, and reported at the Emperor's study. As he awaited the summons to enter, what was his surprise to see coming from the imperial sanctum his old friend Pierre, the deputy doorkeeper of La Force!

"What, Pierre! You in the palace!" he cried.

"And why not, young Desnouettes?" the deputy doorkeeper replied. "Others than pages are sometimes here. As for me — I had an appointment with the Emperor!"

"That is good!" Philip exclaimed heartily. "I hope he did something fine for you. I thought he might. I spoke to him about you."

"Thanks, Monsieur the Page! I am yours forever"; and the deputy doorkeeper bowed so very low that Philip was not certain whether it was in thanks or in fun. A queer little smile, too, played about the corner of the big boy's mouth. "Some day, my Philip," he said, "I may do as much for you. The Emperor thinks well of me, and I may yet get my step. He has given me a special service. What? Oh, we shall see; and so, too, some day may you. Adieu!"

Then he passed on; and even while Philip was puzzling over his hint the summons came, and the page entered the Emperor's study.

"So! you are there, young Desnouettes. And how old are you now, you boy?" This was the Emperor's greeting.

"I shall be sixteen next February, Sire," the boy replied.

"And now it is August. Sixteen is some months away yet," the Emperor said. "But yet, sixteen is coming—and sixteen is the age for effort. See, you Philip! Championship is excellent. Did I not one day make you champion in ordinary to the Emperor? You are a loyal knight; but sometimes championship embarrasses. You were unwise last night. But you were plucky, and pluck is what the boys of France need, if France is to profit by their service. I shall send you to Alfort."

"To Alfort, Sire!" the boy cried.

"Yes—to Alfort, Sire," mimicked the Emperor. "But not to doctor horses, or to feel the pulses of pigs, Monsieur the Page. You shall join the cavalry class, and learn how to ride, and how to care for horses, as one should who, in time, may become a special aide to the Emperor."

"Oh, Sire, you are too good!" exclaimed delighted Philip. "It is what I most desire."

"See, then," said the Emperor, "that you give attention to your duties, and heed the instruction of those set apart to make a man of you. For there are men, my friend, who really do know more than boys, though I sometimes feel that my pages know all there is to know—or think they do."

So Philip went to Alfort, and in that institution, since made into a great veterinary college, the page spent several months, learning the nature and needs of horses. With thirty other boys he received instruction in the cavalry class, and became a daring and expert horseman. The Polytechnic School also he entered, as a "special," to perfect himself in drawing, in topography, and in penmanship; for the Emperor had, evidently, special service in view for this protégé of his, who, in spite of his propensity for getting into scrapes, was honest, plucky, and loyal—the three things that would best combine to make a faithful follower of the Emperor.

A pleasant thing about Alfort was its nearness to Vincennes, where Peyrolles was stationed as one of the drill-masters of the Pupils of the Guard. Philip frequently visited the Corporal, and often, on "leave days," he took the veteran to his friends in the Street of the Fight, where he would listen with glee to the worshiper of the Emperor, and the hater of the Corsican, as they debated long and loud over their pet topic—Napoleon.

"Cæsar has become Charlemagne," Uncle Fauriel declared; "and the republic is dead, indeed. Why was I not a Brutus years ago? Now—alas!—I am too fat to be deliverer or conspirator."

Mademoiselle and Philip laughed merrily over the idea of so fat a Brutus, though Brutus was quite a portly person, Uncle Fauriel informed them. As for Peyrolles, he played a good second to Fauriel's grumbling. "Why did I leave a leg at Austerlitz?" he cried. "Was it to let another man step into the shoes I could no longer wear, and be made the duke or marshal I might have become?"

"Never mind, my Peyrolles," said Philip. "You are drill-master at Vincennes. You are helping to make dukes and marshals for France out of your little Pupils of the Guard."

"Not so easy, that," said the Corporal, shaking his head. "I tried to make of you, young Desnouettes, at St. Cyr, a duke, or at least a marshal—and behold you! only a page yet, or perhaps a horse-doctor!"

"Which may not be so bad a profession after all, Old Mustache," cried Uncle Fauriel. "For what is the saying: 'Set a beggar on horseback, and he will ride to destruction.' The Corsican is mounted already; if Philip will but keep his horses in good trim, the tyrant will ride all the speedier to the end all true patriots most desire. And out of all this may spring a new France, a greater republic. Good Doctor Philip, look to your horses' hoofs."

The Emperor, indeed, was mounted and riding: no one yet could say to what end. For, as 1811 grew into 1812, the war-cloud swelled in bigness, and darkened. In June, 1812, it burst. Napoleon crossed the river Niemen with half a million men. To cross that river in arms was to break the peace: France and Russia were at war.

During the spring months of 1812 the Emperor had drunk deep of power; and Philip, too, from the Emperor's cup had drunk deep of glory. For, though on the eve of a war that was to embroil all Europe, Napoleon sought, first, to dazzle all Europe with his splendor, his resources, and his power. Six hundred thousand men followed the imperial eagles—the mightiest army since the days of Alexander. He set out for the war encompassed by glittering soldiers, and attended by princes and kings. At Dresden he spent three weeks in a blaze of display, marshaling his host. Receptions, festivals, levees, audiences, balls, reviews, shows, and ceremonials crowded each other in dizzy succession; everywhere orders gleamed and diamonds blazed; and where he who once had starved himself as a sub-lieutenant now held state as a monarch, sovereign princes flocked to do honor to this "Marvel of the Age," and vassal kings stood as sup-

164   A BOY OF THE FIRST EMPIRE

pliants in the palace of him whom men called "The New Agamemnon."

Amid all this homage, Napoleon kept his head. While the French served him with idolatry, and the Allies with

"NAPOLEON PULLED THE PAGE'S HAIR VIGOROUSLY IN APPRECIATION OF THE JOKE."

adulation, he sought to give no visible sign of superiority; he could even see the funny side of it all. For one day Philip the page, delaying an answer he should have brought with speed, met the Emperor's impatient demand: "How, then, you page! what are your legs for? Why are you late?"

True to his habit, Philip straightway told the truth.

"Sire," he replied, "I could not help it. I came with the answer straight. But out here in the antechamber I got tangled up in a lot of kings, and had to just crowd my way through them to get in."

Whereat Napoleon laughed, and pulled the boy's ear and hair so vigorously, in his appreciation of the joke, that the tears fairly started in the page's eyes.

For, as you see, Philip was in the thick of it all. Recalled from his studies to grace the progress to Dresden as one of the imperial pages, the boy Philip had been a part of the display that attended it, and, much to his disgust, was sent back to Paris when the Emperor sounded the advance "On to Moscow!" and the Empress returned, by way of Prague, to her palace in France.

In France there was much unrest. The Emperor was fifteen hundred miles away, and nearly every household had been drawn upon for soldiers to fight against Russia. At first came tidings of victories. Then bulletins fell off; news came less regularly; anxiety and rumors filled the air. None knew what to believe; and though, from the heart of Russia, Napoleon ruled France, the people of France were uneasy, and wished their Emperor were back again, with all the brave Frenchmen whom he had led to the war.

But to Philip, dividing his time between his special studies at the Polytechnic School and his duties as a page of the palace, there came but little of this unrest. While the fathers and mothers of France were waiting anxiously for bulletins, sticking pins in their maps of Russia at every place mentioned in the news that came home, and thus following the advance of the troops, the boys of France were puffed up with glory, and longing for the day when they might be old enough to join the Young Guard, and march to victory with their never-conquered Emperor. Philip's only feeling of uneasiness lay in the fear that the war might close before the Emperor should summon him to the field. Indeed, he plead hard for permission to go east on special service, when a relay of couriers bore from the palace of Versailles to the camp before Moscow a gift the Emperor would prize the most,— the portrait of his dearly-loved son, the little King of Rome.

Philip coveted that mission. It would bring him into the heart of the war; it would carry him close to his Emperor; it would call from the lips of the man from whom praise sounded sweetest, thanks and commendation.

But Philip could not have his will in this. Other swift riders than the heedless page bore the precious gift from the heart of France to the heart of Russia, and Philip heard, alike with interest and envy, how delighted with the portrait Napoleon had been, how royally the couriers were thanked, and how, in the camp, the portrait of the baby King was publicly displayed, while all about and before it gathered the grizzled veterans of many battle-fields to admire and do homage to the baby son of their "Little Corporal."

So, when this desire failed him, Philip was certain that the Russians would be completely conquered before he could even have "a drive at them." This fear he confided often to Corporal Peyrolles, and almost as frequently to Mademoiselle.

Peyrolles applauded "my boy," as he called Philip; but Mademoiselle was full of anxieties, conjured alike from Citizen Daunou's gloomy forebodings and young Philip's extravagant notions.

These occupied her thoughts one bright October morning in this year of 1812, when, accompanied by her old nurse, Marcel, now grown into a sort of chaperon to the young girl who had been her charge from babyhood, she set out for a walk from the Street of the Fight to the straggling Street of the Suburb of St. Anthony. For, in that quarter of the city, in the funny old streets (long since swept away by change) known as the Pig-sty and the Tree of Cracow, lived certain poor pensioners, to whom Mademoiselle was a helpful angel of mercy.

She had passed the towering plaster elephant of the Bastille (that ambitious memorial of tyranny overthrown, designed by the Emperor, but never to be changed into bronze as he intended), and had almost reached the dingy side street known as the Little Picpus, when a carriage, dashing furiously down the Street of St. Anthony, almost overturned her as she was picking her way across the foaming gutter; for it had rained heavily in Paris the night before.

Bulky Nurse Marcel caught at the girl's arm. Before she had done so, however, an alert young fellow, stockily built, caught Mademoiselle's other arm, and drew her back to the pavement and Nurse Marcel's care. But while her rescuer had one eye for the girl, he had, also, another for the occupant of the hurrying carriage.

"So, Mademoiselle," he said, "that was a narrow escape. And you could have secured no redress, had you been hurt. It was the carriage of the Prefect of the Seine. He rides as if sent for. Something is afoot."

"Thank you so much," Mademoiselle said prettily. "I

did not see him coming. Even when one is sent for, one need not ride so furiously, and scare people half out of their wits."

"Ah, Mademoiselle," the boy declared with amusing importance, "when one is, like us, in an official station, one must do many things that do not seem gentle—even to running down pretty girls, out for an airing."

"Mademoiselle,— to me!" came Nurse Marcel's warning voice. But Mademoiselle was inquisitive, and was now determined to hear more from this young official.

"And you are an official, then, Monsieur?" she asked the big boy.

"A deputy doorkeeper at La Force, Mademoiselle," he replied.

"La Force? the prison? Then you must know Pierre. I mean Pierre Labeau—a boy on duty there."

"I am that Pierre Labeau, at your service, Mademoiselle. And you?"

"Oh, we have heard of you so often from Philip! Have we not, Nurse? This is Monsieur Philip's friend, Pierre."

"And a very forward young man he is!" cried Nurse Marcel. "Come away with me at once, Mademoiselle."

"Monsieur Philip!" cried Pierre. "Is it, then, young Desnouettes, the page, of whom you speak? Then you— you, Mademoiselle, perhaps, are—"

"Mademoiselle Lucie Daunou, of the Street of the Fight," said the girl.

"But not Citizen Daunou's daughter—is she now, Nurse?" Pierre demanded, so quickly, indeed, that Nurse Marcel flushed, and said sharply, "And why not? Who else, Monsieur Stupid? Why, I have known her ever since the day

Citizen Daunou brought her to his home—bah, then! what am I saying?" she cried in startled confusion.

"Brought me—me! Why, what are you saying, Nurse? What does it mean, that?" Mademoiselle cried. "I never heard of it! Oh! but what is this?"

It was a bit of torn paper blown by the wind into the girl's hand. Even in her surprise at Nurse Marcel's words, Mademoiselle's curiosity as to the bit of torn paper displaced her first inquisitiveness, and she spread it out to read.

It was baffling; for this is what she saw:

> *To the Count Frochut, Prefect*
> *he Seine, wherever he may be found.*
> *Ride with speed!*
>   GENERAL HEADQUARTERS,
>   PLACE VENDÔME.
>   23d October, 1812,
>   6 o'clock, A. M.
> REFECT.— I have the honor to
> py of the decree of the Sen-
>   nouncing the sad ti-
>   of the Emperor, by a
>   walls of Moscow on
>   of this month of October
>   on of their command,
>   e the City Hall for
>   provisional gov-
>   the Republic
>   th speed.
>   LET.
>   Army of
>   Paris.

"'WHAT IS THAT, PIERRE?' SHE SAID, POINTING TO THE WORDS."

"How strange!" cried Mademoiselle. "What can it all mean, Pierre?"

The deputy doorkeeper, equally curious, took the letter, and scanned it curiously.

"'The Count Frochat, Prefect of the Seine,'" he read. "It came from his carriage then, Mademoiselle—'decree of of the Senate—announcing sad tidings—of the Emperor—walls of Moscow—month of October—the City Hall—provisional government—the Republic—Army of Paris'—why, what is it, then? I said something was up. Something is!"

He turned the torn paper over, puzzled enough. Mademoiselle's sharp eyes caught sight of some bold handwriting on the back of the letter.

"What is that, Pierre?" she said, pointing to the words.

"*Fu—it*," the boy spelled out. "I do not know, Mademoiselle. It is not French, this. What is it?"

It was not French. It was Latin. Mademoiselle read the two bold words, looking over Pierre's shoulder. "'*Fuit Imperator!*' That means, 'The Emperor has been.' The Emperor has been? Oh, Pierre! What have I found?" she cried. "The Emperor is dead!"

Pierre excitedly struck his hand upon the torn bit of paper.

"So! I see it all!" he cried. "Killed under the walls of Moscow! Whew! but here is a tangle, though!"

And without a word of adieu the deputy doorkeeper turned sharply, and dashed down the Street of the Suburb of St. Anthony, heading as straight as its crowded ways would permit for the City Hall and the "General Headquarters" in the Place Vendôme.

CHAPTER XIV

WHY PHILIP WAS MAD AT THE CLERK OF THE WEATHER

MADEMOISELLE stood for a moment looking after the flying Pierre. Then she said: "Oh, that poor little baby! Why, he is emperor now! Come with me, Nurse. I must go to the palace and tell Philip. Perhaps he does not know it, and he might wish to hear of it in time."

"But we are not for palaces, Mademoiselle," Nurse Marcel objected. "How would I be received there—I, the widow of a sansculotte? They will send me to La Force, if they do but know that once I was 'Citizeness' and danced the Carmagnole."

"Never fear that, Nurse," Mademoiselle reassured her companion. "They cannot know; and I—I must see Philip."

So, grumbling still, Nurse Marcel turned with the young girl, and together they hastened westward; for, though the Empress was at St. Cloud, Philip's duties were largely at the Tuileries when he was not at the Polytechnic School.

Mademoiselle saw that soldiers were marching that way, and that in the City Hall Square the whole Tenth Cohort was drawn up before the city building. Clearly something had happened.

At the palace Mademoiselle soon found Philip. To him

she told the news. Had he heard it? she asked. Was it not dreadful?

"Dreadful? Why, it is never true," Philip declared. "The bullet is not made that can kill the Emperor. The letter was a trick. Wait here a moment, Mademoiselle. Let me report what you tell me, and inquire."

He returned speedily.

"Something *is* wrong," he said. "The square is filling with soldiers. The horse-guards have just galloped to St. Cloud. Every one seems mystified. Strange things, they say, have happened. The Minister of Police has been locked up in La Force. So, too, has Pasquier, the prefect. The commander of the Paris garrison has been assassinated. The City Hall is surrounded; the Ministry of War is in the hands of the republicans; the Senate, it is said, has issued a decree announcing the death of the Emperor, and proclaiming the Republic."

"The Republic!" exclaimed Mademoiselle. "Why, Philip, how may that be? If the Emperor is dead, the little King of Rome is Emperor. Why should the republicans have the power? Dear me! I hope my father is not in it all. Of course Uncle Fauriel is."

"For all they say, I will not believe it," Philip declared. "The Emperor dead! How absurd! The Emperor cannot die. What would become of France?"

"Why, Philip, I suppose emperors have died before," Mademoiselle suggested.

"But not *The* Emperor," said Philip, proudly. "But, true or not, I am in a muddle; and what a ferment will France be in! So, too, will the city. Were it not wise, Mademoiselle, for me to conduct you, and Nurse here, to the Street of the Fight—or at least to Citizen Daunou's safe-keeping in the Archives? The streets will soon be in an uproar."

So, dodging the crowds that thronged the streets, and yet, with the curiosity of youth, unwilling to let slip any chance of seeing what was afoot, the young people, with Nurse Marcel clutching at Mademoiselle's arm, arrived at last at the Palace of the Archives in the Street of the Wheat-field.

There, in his office, they found the good Keeper of the Archives, as cool and as calm as ever, poring over his dusty documents, and apparently indifferent to all the rumors and excitement that filled the city.

Breathless, they told what Mademoiselle had found, and what Philip had heard.

"The Emperor dead? That is now but ancient history, my children," remarked the old Keeper. "Was I in it? No; nor yet Uncle Fauriel. Do you take us for lunatics, you two? Why, it was but a scare and a sell. And yet, it might have proved a tragedy—that I will admit. But, bless you both! the Emperor is as alive as you or I; and the hot-heads, the crazy-pates, who sought to raise an insurrection, are safe, now, under lock and key. Yes, it was nearly accomplished —that I may not deny; but by a lucky chance—or shall we say an unlucky one?—who can tell?—by a lucky chance, let us call it, the plot failed; and thanks to whom, think you? To your friend Pierre, my Philip—Pierre, the deputy door-keeper of La Force. He is the hero of the hour. I have but just heard the whole story. That crazy-pate Malet, late general under the Republic,—you must have heard Uncle Fauriel tell of him,—was at the bottom of it all; and now he is in prison once more, and his life is not worth a button. So, come, get you back to home and duty, my children. It is but an incident. See—it is over. Leave me to my papers."

Citizen Daunou was right. It was but an incident, but it well-nigh proved an event. A cleverly laid plot against the Empire, which included an announcement of the Emperor's death, a forged decree of the Senate, a surprise of the heads of departments, and the transfer of all commands to the conspirators, had been so skilfully carried out that it would have succeeded but for the quick eye of Pierre, the deputy doorkeeper of La Force.

The account of the attempt is one of the most dramatic chapters in the Napoleonic story; but, save for Pierre's connection with it, the conspiracy of General Malet, as it is called, has no especial bearing upon our narrative. It was one of those historic oddities that might have changed the world's history had it succeeded. But it failed; and, to-day, it is almost forgotten, though certain foolish and certain brave men paid with their lives for their connection with it.

Philip lost no time in hunting up Pierre at La Force. From him he learned the details of that lynx-eyed young fellow's part in the drama.

"After I left Mademoiselle," the deputy doorkeeper said, "I hurried to the City Hall. I could learn nothing certain; but that homely little commander Laborde—you know him, my Philip, that bunged-up aide-de-camp of Doucet the adjutant—he spied me. 'Here, then, you Labeau, come with me to headquarters,' he said; 'you may be of service to me.' You see, he knew I was on duty at La Force, and I suppose he thought if he should happen to be arrested and sent there, it would be well to be in my care. So to headquarters we went—in the Place Vendôme. The troops were all about the building, and the sentries would not let us pass. Our little Laborde cried: 'Fools! I am here on duty. Let me enter.' And they did. We went to the adjutant's office. Laborde left me without. I heard high words. Then Laborde called me. I broke past the sentry at the door, and entered. Doucet the adjutant was there; Laborde was there; a man in a general's uniform was there. I looked at him. I knew him. 'What, General Malet!' I said, 'you here? Who gave you leave to quit La Force!' My faith, Philip! He was one of my prisoners—Malet the republican, from the prison hospital. Oh, but he was mad! 'Fool!' he hissed at me. 'Fool, yourself!' said I. 'Here is something wrong, gentlemen. This is an escaped prisoner. Arrest him, and I will go for the Minister of Police.' With that, the runaway tried to pull his pistol. We jumped at him and pinned him down. 'An escaped lunatic?' asked Doucet the adjutant, as he sat on the fallen general. 'And the decree of the Senate?' he asked. 'Forged, Monsieur the Adjutant,' I said; 'it must be a forged decree. This Malet is a clever lunatic.' Laborde ran to the window. 'A trick! a trick!' he cried. 'The Emperor is not dead. To your barracks, soldiers! The Emperor lives, I say! You have been sold by a lunatic!' That is all there is to it, my Philip. The plot is discovered. The scare is over. Malet is in La Force, and I—"

"You have saved France, Pierre," Philip cried, hugging the deputy doorkeeper in delight.

"Well—perhaps. Thanks to your Mademoiselle Daunou

—if she is Daunou," said Pierre. "If Mademoiselle had not found that bit of torn paper in the Street of St. Anthony, I should not have been on hand; I should not have recognized Malet; he would have succeeded, and—whew, though! what a tangle we should have been in!"

Philip felt proud of his friends. Mademoiselle and Pierre had saved the Empire, and won the thanks of the Emperor.

"Long life to both of you!" he cried. "Pierre, you will get your step."

Pierre did get his step. For when the Emperor returned to Paris, Pierre was made a police inspector,—the youngest on the force,—and he received the thanks of the Emperor.

"You were the only one, you boy," said Napoleon, "among all those imbeciles in power, that had eyes, and could see: that had brains, and could use them. I said you were clever. I was right. My faith! if you were but old enough I would make you Minister of Police. You are the best duke among them all."

For, you see, Napoleon did come back. That coming back is historic. The world has not yet finished talking of it.

Philip was on hand when it happened. It was December 18, in that eventful year of 1812. Paris was depressed. France was distressed. The world was astonished. Only the day before there had been made public a bulletin from the army in Russia, in which the Emperor told France that he had not succeeded in conquering Russia. He had not lost a battle. His soldiers had been brave and heroic. But the weather had proved their enemy. The cold had been so intense that men and horses had perished. Order had been lost. Woe and disaster fell upon the armies of France. The Cossacks had harried them. In recrossing the Beresina River many had been drowned. But the Emperor was alive and well.

Men shook their heads gravely over this unexpected news. But boys are ever hopeful. Philip had said: "Ah! the Emperor is there. He will soon set matters right." And he had thought but little of disaster. For his Emperor had never known defeat! He never could know it!

It was half-past eleven o'clock on the night of December 18. Philip was on duty at the Tuileries. At his post outside the drawing-room of the Empress he sat nodding, half asleep.

Suddenly he started to his feet. The sound of voices in dispute, as if demanding an entrance, came to his ears. They were in the corridor below him, at the very entrance to the palace.

The door of the antechamber in which the listening page was stationed was flung open. Two men hurried in. They were wrapped in furs, and looked rough and excited.

"Is it a new plot?" Philip wondered. Beyond him were the apartments of the Empress and the little King of Rome —the heir to the Empire. Philip's breath came fast. His heart beat excitedly. He was but a boy, he thought, but he would defend the Empress with his life.

"Stand back, sirs!" he cried. "This is the apartment of the Empress. None may enter here!"

He had no weapon at hand, but he caught up a chair, and threatened the strangers, blocking their advance.

"What, boy! Why, young Desnouettes," cried the smaller of the two men, "do you not know me?"

It was the Emperor! Philip almost dropped in surprise.

"'STAND BACK, SIRS,' HE CRIED. 'THIS IS THE APARTMENT OF THE EMPRESS!'"

"You, Sire?" he exclaimed in amazement. "And the Russians? Are they defeated already!"

"Already?" the Emperor repeated, almost sadly, placing a hand upon the boy's head. "We are alone. You are a brave boy, you Philip. Come, Cauliancourt."

And, without another word, the Emperor and his equerry pushed past the page, and entered the drawing-room of the Empress.

Philip was puzzled. The Emperor? and alone? He could not understand it all.

But too soon he did. And so did France. Napoleon had suffered his first defeat.

Of all that vast army, the fugitive Emperor was the only man who had yet returned. Thousands upon thousands of brave Frenchmen had left their bones bleaching upon Russian snows. Of the half-million men who with streaming banners and flashing bayonets had crossed the Niemen to conquer the East, only a paltry seventy thousand recrossed—a tattered, frost-bitten, starving, straggling, desperate, and weary band of defeated fugitives. The invasion of Russia was a terrible failure.

It was the cold that had done it. The Clerk of the Weather had taken the field against Napoleon, and the unconquered Emperor had been vanquished by the thermometer.

That was what he declared. That was what Philip accepted; and, with many a sigh and many a bitter thought, the boy, who believed so firmly in the prowess and puissance of his Emperor, blamed the Clerk of the Weather and cried, "Hard luck! This General Frost is a beast! If only, now, the weather were a man, how the Emperor would have beaten him!"

Poor Philip; poor France; poor Emperor! Malet's conspiracy and Russian frosts were to begin a new chapter in the history of their homeland, and bring, to all three, changes and adventures of which none of them had ever dreamed.

CHAPTER XV

THE PRISONER OF FONTAINEBLEAU

IN the days of discussion that followed the Emperor's return from Russia, Philip found his greatest comfort in Corporal Peyrolles. The veteran of Austerlitz would come stumping along the Street of the Fight, and in the quiet home of the Keeper of the Archives would second all Philip's extravagant claims as to the invincibleness of the Emperor, and would "have it out" with Uncle Fauriel, who pretended to see in the Russian disaster the vengeance of Heaven on the "Corsican ogre" who had, so he said, "betrayed the Republic."

"Did I leave a leg at Austerlitz," demanded Corporal Peyrolles, "to drag the other around after a defeated Emperor? No, Citizen! It was to have one good leg left, with which to dance in joy over every victory. And let me tell you, I can dance on one leg better than some of those dukes and marshals at the palace can on two—with all their titles. Faith! but I can, Mademoiselle. See, now!" and, catching Mademoiselle round the waist, the old fellow actually swung the girl about the room, humming meanwhile one of the lively airs of the camp, to keep step to. Then, while the others applauded, they sank into chairs, the Corporal panting and Mademoiselle laughing merrily.

"You see, Peyrolles is good for something yet," said the Corporal. "And as for the leg, Citizen," he cried to Uncle Fauriel, "it has been a good republican leg; yes, I grant you that. But it was a good First Consulate leg; and it is a good Empire leg, too. For, look you, it is the Emperor's leg!" and he slapped his one sound limb so heartily that Mademoiselle and Philip laughed aloud, and the page cried enthusiastically, "Long live the leg! Corporal Peyrolles's one is better than the Czar's million!"

"True for you, my Philip!" said the Corporal. "What is a Cossack's leg good for but to run away with? or a Prussian's? or an Englisher's? or the leg of any enemy of the Emperor? I said to the Little Corporal the night before Marengo—I stood on guard in front of his tent that night—'General,' I said, 'strike 'em on the flank, and they'll run with all the legs they have left.' And they did! 'Peyrolles,' said the Little Corporal to me the night after Marengo—I was on guard before his tent that night, too—'Peyrolles,' he said, 'your advice was good. Did you see 'em run?' 'I did, my General,' said I, 'I knew they would. Do you keep at it, and you will have all Europe running.' And, my faith! run they have. From that day to this."

"But the Corsican's legs are sound yet, my Corporal," said Uncle Fauriel, "and he is running too. He is running to destruction, and dragging all France with him."

"Bah!" cried Corporal Peyrolles. "It is the home-made dukes and marshals who are running that way—if any one is—with their thirst for titles and their greed for riches. Reduce 'em to the ranks, I say; reduce 'em to the ranks! and put true men in their place—even if they should be one-legged ones. Then I'll back the Little Corporal against all Europe, and Russia in the bargain."

For Corporal Peyrolles would never admit that the Russians were Europeans. "They're Cossacks," he said; "and a Cossack is a pagan. Scratch him, and every time you'll find a Tartar underneath. That's what the Emperor says, and so say I."

But Citizen Daunou said: "Ah, my friends, it is not a question of France and her salvation. If the Emperor will but be warned by this Russian disaster; if he will but heed the wail going up from thousands of French homes; if he will but keep friendship with Austria or Prussia or the Confederates of the Rhine; if he will but remember that a single card may lose as well as win the game, France may not need to stand at bay against all Europe; and both the Empire and the Emperor may be saved. It is wise, when your ship is drifting toward the breakers, to throw something overboard, and thus save ship and cargo. But, alas! the Emperor never was anything of a sailor. He will crowd on sail, and head straight for the rocks."

Philip did not believe this. He thought his old friend was what to-day we call an "alarmist." Philip was, indeed, a boy of the Empire. He had faith in Napoleon as the greatest man in all the world. To him Napoleon was France; France was the Empire; and the Empire would one day be Europe. So, as much as any boy cares to think on such questions, Philip thought the future was clear. He believed that the Russian campaign had, indeed, been a victory. Did not Napoleon plant the eagles on the walls of Moscow? And what is that but victory? He knew that the Emperor would yet humble Europe, punish Russia, and give new glory to France as conqueror and as ruler.

On January 1, 1813, at the Emperor's New Year's day reception, Philip saw only the greatness and glory of Napoleon. Alike at review and fête that ushered in that disastrous year for France, this optimistic and vivacious young page was full of boastfulness as to the Emperor's invincibleness and "the Emperor's luck."

France was arming again. Almost drained of men for the struggle with Russia, she was now girding herself anew for a death-grapple with all Europe. Old men and young men, veterans and boys, filled the ranks. The shattered regiments were refilled. The Young Guard, drawn from the freshest blood of France, was formed into squadrons and battalions in blue; and Napoleon, looking at his new fighting-men that France had given him, cried with pleasure as they passed in review before him: "Ah, with these one may conquer every one and everywhere!"

The Emperor was continually on the go in those busy days. And so, too, was Philip. For the page, growing in strength and favor, was constantly in attendance on the Emperor at the palaces, in the city, at the hunt, and in the home apartments.

Here, on a certain January day, as he was helping the Emperor put on his coat of green and gold, Philip overheard Napoleon say to his confidant, the Marshal of the Palace: "To-morrow we hunt at Grosbois, Duroc. We must keep moving. I must be active, so that the newspapers will talk of it, and the English, who say I am sick, will see that they lie. Sick! I never was better, Duroc. But I am getting too fat, my friend, and action makes one thinner. Have patience. I will soon show Europe that I am the healthiest man alive."

There was no doubt as to the truth of this statement. The Emperor was growing fat. The thin and sickly-looking conqueror of Arcola and Marengo had grown into the fat and "well-groomed" lord of the land; and even Philip's loyalty could not deny that some day his hero and idol might even be as fat as Uncle Fauriel. But he hoped not.

Philip was glad of the hunting at Grosbois. He revelled in the action and excitement of the chase, and could manage to cover more ground, and be in more places at once, than any page of his size in the imperial train. So he was on hand betimes next morning when, with but a few attendants, the Emperor rode toward the barriers, on his way to join the Empress and certain of the court at Grosbois, the estate of Prince Berthier, near Melun, some thirty miles from Paris.

As they rode along the crowded Street of the Suburb of St. Anthony,—that street in which Mademoiselle had found the famous bit of torn paper that had led to the knowledge of Malet's plot,—Philip saw a boy not much older than himself spring from the watching crowd straight in the Emperor's path.

"Is it, then, an assassination?" Philip asked himself. "The Emperor is in danger!" And, quick as thought, he sprang from his horse and seized the boy's arm.

But the Emperor said: "Hold, there, young Desnouettes! What do you wish, you boy?"

"My freedom!" cried the boy. "See! your boy-stealers have drawn me to fight against the Cossacks. What do I care for the Cossacks? My old mother is more to me. What do I care for your throne? My home is dearer. My mother needs me more than you do. If I go, she starves. If I am killed, she dies. Hands off, palace-cub, Nicholas-dog!" he cried to Philip. "I do not seek to kill this Bonaparte. I would kill no one. I would keep my skin for my mother. I am a Paris boy, and too good to feed Russian wolves!"

The police made a dash at this boy who braved the Emperor; but from the crowd came threatening cries: "Touch him not, prison-sheep!" "Yah! Bonaparte!—Nicholas!—give us peace! We have had fighting enough!"

The police faced the crowd. The Emperor sat calm and immovable. Then, with a rush such as is known only to Paris mobs, the crowd made a dash for the prisoner. The police were forced off; Philip was rolled over in the mud, and when he struggled to his feet the boy was gone, while cries of delight and derision came from the victorious crowd. There had been a rescue, and the conscript had been smuggled away by his friends.

And still the Emperor sat immovable. This was a new experience for him. But it was not his policy, just now, to antagonize the people. His success depended upon their agreeing to his demands.

"Let the boy go," he said. "The fools do not know what they want. A mob is but a pig, and you police—bah! you are imbeciles. To horse, my page; ride on, gentlemen! And you,"—this to the discomfited police,—"let not this thing happen again."

Bent on his purpose, Napoleon would not listen to the voice of his people. They might be tired of war; so, too, was he. But with one end in view—supremacy—he could ignore both his own and the people's wish. Incidents like this had, therefore, but little weight with him. "It is but a yell of the mob," he said; "I will quiet it by a victory. My hope is in my army."

So they rode on to Grosbois—the "great wood" where was the villa of Prince Berthier, that dragoon captain who had fought for American freedom under Lafayette, had defended King Louis of France in the days of the Terror, and had helped Bonaparte win his way to a throne. And there, on the edge of the great forest of Fontainebleau, they hunted the boar that January afternoon, and Philip had a glorious time.

Flushed with the excitement of the chase, he rode hither and thither, in close attendance on the Emperor. This touch of danger and uncertainty just suited the boy.

But once, when the prickers had driven the big boar straight toward the imperial spear, Philip was surprised to see the Emperor, forgetful of the sport, with his head bent and his reins slack on his horse's neck, lost in thought.

"On guard, Sire!" cried the page. "The pig will escape you." And, fearing this, he dashed forward to head off the beast and drive him back for the Emperor's spear.

"Eh? So, boy! I was thinking. I had the Prussians almost cornered. Kill the pig yourself."

Philip sought to do this, but he had lost his chance. His horse turned about sharply; the boar, darting between the horse's legs, disconcerted the steed; it snorted, reared, and plunged, and over on his head went Monsieur the Page. The boar turned to charge, and the Emperor, now aroused from his reverie, at once saw the boy's danger. Spurring his horse to the spot, with an expert plunge of the spear he ran the boar through, just as its murderous tusks were within an ace of impaling the prostrate page.

"Why, Philip; why, boy!" cried the Emperor; "your training at Alfort must have been poor. Can you not keep your saddle better than that? How can you expect, then, to ride a cavalry charge?"

Philip rose, feeling very small indeed. Thrown by a mob! Thrown by a pig! This was not exactly a day of laurels for Monsieur the Page. But the Emperor cried gaily: "'T is the fortune of war, young Desnouettes! Up and try it again!" and, much chagrined at his clumsiness, Philip mounted his horse and dropped behind the Emperor.

Next morning the talk at the grand breakfast in the castle of Grosbois was all of the hunt that was planned for the day. Horses and huntsmen were in readiness when, suddenly, the Emperor sprang a surprise upon the company.

"Ladies and gentlemen," he said, "we shall not hunt to-day. We ride to Fontainebleau."

"To Fontainebleau, Sire!" cried the ladies in dismay. "To Fontainebleau? Why, we have only our hunting-dresses with us!"

"I weep for you, ladies," said the Emperor, in mock sympathy; "but such are my plans. The Holy Father will, I am sure, excuse your hunting-dress. Boy Philip, is the post-chaise ready for me?"

"It waits in the court, Sire," Philip replied.

"Good," said the Emperor. "Do you, then, mount your horse and gallop on ahead to the palace. Tell Monsieur the

THE PRISONER OF FONTAINEBLEAU 191

THE EMPEROR SAVES PHILIP FROM THE BOAR.

Chamberlain that I shall be there within the hour. But let him on no account acquaint the Holy Father of my coming. Now, then, off with speed! Ride on, boy; ride on!"

It was well that Philip had snatched a hasty bit to eat that morning with the chief page of Prince Berthier. Otherwise he would have gone breakfastless. For he was on his horse in an instant, galloping through the forest to the palace at Fontainebleau, where, for more than a year, the Emperor had held a close prisoner that Pope of Rome known as Pius the Seventh.

The quarrel between the Emperor and the Pope has no bearing on our story. Suffice it to say that when Napoleon assumed the sovereignty of Italy he took away from the Pope what is known as his temporal power—the right to rule the States of the Church as a landed prince. And when that spirited old Pontiff objected to Napoleon's ways, the Emperor stole him bodily—first from Rome, and then from Savona, until finally he shut the Pope up in this palace of Fontainebleau until such time as the Holy Father would yield to the imperial will. This the Pope refused to do; and, living the life of a recluse in that great gilded palace, he had come to be known to men as the Prisoner of Fontainebleau.

Through the crisp winter's morning Philip rode on to Fontainebleau. Into the wide forest he galloped; on under its great leafless trees; on past the meadows, lawns, and cliffs that make the forest of Fontainebleau one of the world's picture-spots; on past the Cross of the Specter Huntsman, the Gorge of the Wolf, the Pool of the Elves, the Miraculous Weeping Rock, and the Robbers' Cave, up the Grand Promenade of the Queen, and so through the great gardens into the splendid Court of the White Horse. Here he threw his reins to the groom, and sought in the palace Monsieur the Captain Lagrosse of the Imperial Guard, who, while really the jailer, posed as the chamberlain of the Prisoner of Fontainebleau.

Philip delivered his message. At once there was the bustle

of preparation. Not for a year and more had the Emperor or his court been seen at the great palace.

Philip, left to his own devices, wandered through the splendid building, prying into the magnificent rooms, in which kings and queens had held high festival in days gone by and wondering, boy-like, as he peeped and pried, in just what rooms the captive Pope of Rome lived in priestly state.

Along a wide hall that looked out upon the Court of the Fountain, Philip strolled and loitered, trying door after door in his curiosity. One of these opened to his touch, and the page, passing through, found himself in a little room that looked like a very plain and poorly furnished bed-chamber. Within the room a spare and pleasant-faced man sat, busy with needle and thread, mending a pair of breeches.

"Eh, there! Grandfather," cried the heedless page. "I knew no one was here. Could you tell me, you now, where one might see the prisoner?"

"The prisoner, my son?" the old man repeated, looking at the boy in gentle inquiry.

"I mean the Pope, the Pope Pius," explained Philip; "he whom men call the Prisoner of Fontainebleau."

"I am that unfortunate, my son," said the old man, rising. "What would you with me? Speak. I am the Pope."

"You the Pope! You—and in this mean little room— mending old clothes like that! Oh, Father—your Holiness, forgive me! I—I did not know—" and down on his knees before this sweet-faced old man dropped the prying page, now deeply mortified at his heedlessness of speech and act.

CHAPTER XVI

FOR FRANCE

AT that moment a voice was heard in the outer room into which the prisoner's apartment opened; then came the sound of swinging doors and hurrying feet.

The Pope, living in an atmosphere of uncertainty, gave quick ear to the disturbance. He drew away his hand from the head of the kneeling boy, and looked with anxious inquiry into Philip's upturned face. Did this boy's presence, this sudden noise of intrusion, mean a new danger for him? Recollections flashed across him of how a conqueror had, in earlier days, dared, with gauntleted hand, to buffet a Pope in the face, and how that very room in which he sat had, long years ago, been the apartment of that stanch Archbishop Thomas à Becket, whom an English king had murdered at the very altar. He threw aside the well-worn breeches he had been mending, and stood erect, defiance and resignation curiously mingled on his face.

Philip, too, sprang to his feet.

"It is the Emperor!" he cried.

"The Emperor?—here?" echoed Pope Pius. He strode to the door and flung it open. There, in the opposite doorway, stood his persecutor and his opponent. But not as a foeman, nor an assassin, did the great Emperor appear. Instead, his broad, handsome face beamed with friendship; from eyes and lips sprang the smiles of welcome and good will. Crossing the Pope's antechamber, which once had been the boudoir of the famous Anne of Austria, the mother of Louis Fourteenth, he almost ran, with extended arms, to where in the open doorway stood the startled Pope, with the troubled page behind him.

Napoleon flung his arms about the Pontiff.

"My father!" he cried, and kissed him on the cheek.

"My son!" the Pope responded, tenderly but with dignity, and returned the embrace and the kiss.

Thus, after years of resistance and persecution, did Pope and Emperor meet. Pope Pius saw only the man whom, ten years before, he had anointed Emperor of the French; Napoleon saw but the man from whose hands he had received the imperial crown, and whom it was now his policy to reconcile; and all seemed lovely once again.

How, even then, the Emperor had his way, and by his own peculiar method forced the Pope to sign, one week later, in that very room, the famous agreement known as the Concordat of Fontainebleau, is history, but not especially a part of our story.

For nearly ten days the court remained at Fontainebleau, though how the Empress and her ladies managed with simply their hunting-dresses as their toilets the record fails to show. But when Napoleon rode back to Paris he had accomplished what his surprise-party to the Pope was intended to achieve.

As for Philip, he experienced for days no little uncertainty and chagrin, although he managed, of course, to have a good time at Fontainebleau, and received many friendly words from the Pope he had so unceremoniously accosted.

He had not made a dazzling success of himself, however, on this semi-official outing. He had been tumbled into the mud when he had tried to protect the Emperor from a fancied assassination; he had been flung heels over head and almost disabled on the hunting-field, when he had the chance to show his valor and his skill; he had intruded most unwarrantably upon the privacy of a Pope, and used language of which he was ashamed. Certainly, as a page of the palace, he had displayed an ability for blundering into scrapes, in which only his loyalty and the Emperor's favor saved him from ridicule and a scolding.

The Emperor saw this, too. For, one day, standing in the gorgeous vestibule that led to the private apartments of the Emperor, Philip was suddenly accosted by Napoleon.

"Well, my Philip," the Emperor said, "you look big enough to be a man. How old now, you boy?"

"Seventeen next August, Sire," said the page.

"Within the legal age for conscription, eh?" queried the Emperor. "And smart and sound enough, although something of a blunderer. We must find active service for you. Sometimes you appear to be more a bull in a china-shop than a quiet page of the palace. But you do your best, you boy; you do your best. We must put your overflow of spirits to better service for France."

For France! That was the Emperor's one thought now; that, too, was Philip's desire, and he hailed with delight the promise of a change of duty.

For France! that was the wish alike of Emperor and people, though opinion as to how France would best be served differed with people and Emperor. With one it meant peace without war; with the other it meant peace through war. And the Emperor generally had his way.

One night, after the return to the Tuileries, the page came with a message, searching for the Emperor. He found him in the rooms of the little King of Rome, just as the imperial two-year-old was being prepared for bed.

The Emperor raised his hand for silence as the page entered the room. The little King was kneeling by his governess, good Madame de Montesquiou, saying his prayers. And as the page waited in the doorway, he heard these words lisped by the baby lips: "Bless my dear papa, O Lord God! and fill him with the desire to make peace for the happiness of France, and of us all."

The Emperor smiled, and laid his hand tenderly on his son's head. He knew that the inspiration of the child's prayer came from the little King's governess, a devout and loyal Frenchwoman.

"I desire peace, my little one, as deeply as does any one in France. But how? but how?" he said; and then, turning to Philip, he demanded his message.

Next day, in the Street of the Fight, Philip told of the little King's prayer, and Citizen Daunou said, solemnly, "Out of the mouths of babes comes, sometimes, the Lord's truth. If but the Emperor would heed it! But, alas! he will not. He has yet to learn the grandeur of the victory through peace. Heaven send he may not learn it at the cost of his crown, his country, and his life!"

Pierre was there that day. The young inspector of police

was becoming a frequent visitor at the house of the Keeper of the Archives, who, like the good republican he was, disdained the distinctions of rank and of title, if but men were true at heart, and welcomed at Mademoiselle's salon all his friends on equal footing and with equal good will.

Pierre beckoned the old Keeper aside.

"I have found something, Citizen Daunou," he said, "that for nearly two years I have been hunting down—at the Emperor's request, mark you. Only to-day did I unearth what may be the thing I seek. I found it—well, no need to tell you where. We of the police have to go underneath as well as overhead, you know. Enough that I have found it. Will you read it, Citizen? See if you can fit it to anything you have."

Citizen Daunou took from Pierre's hand the piece of paper the inspector held out to him. It was a frayed and dingy slip, yellow with age, and with the appearance of having been torn, years before, from a larger document. The old man adjusted his spectacles, and read the words upon the slip. They were not many, but they seemed to startle him. He gave a glance of rapid inquiry at Pierre. Then he read the lines again.

"Why? What is it?" he said. "This is most singular. This is—my faith! Pierre, it may be—it is the missing record! And you found it—where?"

Pierre shrugged his shoulders. "That is my affair, Citizen," he said. "Does it tell you anything?"

Did it not, though? For this is what good Citizen Daunou read on that frayed and dingy bit of paper:

"... —izen Jules Marcel of the Street of the Straight Wall, to bring up as good patriots and as children of the Republic."

NAPOLEON'S VETERANS VIEWING THE PORTRAIT OF THE KING OF ROME.

"Marcel? Marcel? Jules Marcel?" mused Citizen Daunou, tapping his forehead. "Why, that was the husband of Mademoiselle's nurse. He was a sansculotte. And from her must have come— A light! A light! Pierre! I see a light! And the Emperor said I was but an owl! I was, my faith! I was. Will you give me this, lad? I must study it out, and think it over. And—why is it with you?"

"The Emperor's commission, Citizen," said the boy inspector. "He said to me, 'Find this out for me.' And look you, I have found it."

"Have you shown it to him yet?" asked Citizen Daunou.

"No, Citizen," Pierre replied; "for have you not the rest of the paper?"

"To be sure; so I have—at the Archives," the Keeper admitted. "Let me but take this there and fit the pieces together; then may I unravel the tangled threads. I must study it out with certainty. Trust me, you shall have all the glory of the find, my Pierre.

"Oh, as for that, my friend,"—another shrug,—"if it solves the riddle, and does those we know a service, it is glory enough for me. It is my life—such things as this riddle-solving, Citizen."

Citizen Daunou wrung the young inspector's hand. Then he fell upon him, and embraced him with true French enthusiasm.

"You should be minister of police, my Pierre," he said.

"So, once, the Emperor told me," Pierre commented quietly.

"You carry a wise head on those young shoulders of yours," the Keeper of the Archives said. "But more of this matter later. Come to me at the Archives on your next leave day, and together we will study out this mystery."

There was no doubt that Pierre's cleverness had brought about an important result. But so, too, had Philip's loyalty led to results equally important in that young patriot's estimation. For one bright day in March, as he awaited in the Tuileries garden the pleasure of good Madame de Montesquiou, the governess of the little King of Rome, he spied the Emperor pacing the path, head bent, and hands behind his back—his best-remembered attitude.

"So, Monsieur the Page, are you there?" he said. "I have been thinking of you. Almost seventeen, eh? And here is all France rallying around the eagles. It is Young France's opportunity for glory. It shall be yours. And you—you, my Philip," he went on eagerly; "look now! You are nearly seventeen. You are sturdy and strong. Sometimes you play the fool, but you are true-hearted and faithful. You know the ways of palaces. You can read; you can write; you can ride; you can draw plans; you can foot up figures; you can obey orders quickly and with brains. You are too good for a private soldier, or even a sub-lieutenant; you are not good enough for a captain or a private secretary. You shall join my new flying squadron of field secretaries—my unofficial aides-de-camp. You shall go to the wars with me as one of my new officers of ordonnance."

"Oh, Sire! in that splendid uniform of blue and silver?" cried the page.

"Hear the boy!" laughed the Emperor, tweaking the page's ear. "I give him a chance for glory, and he chatters

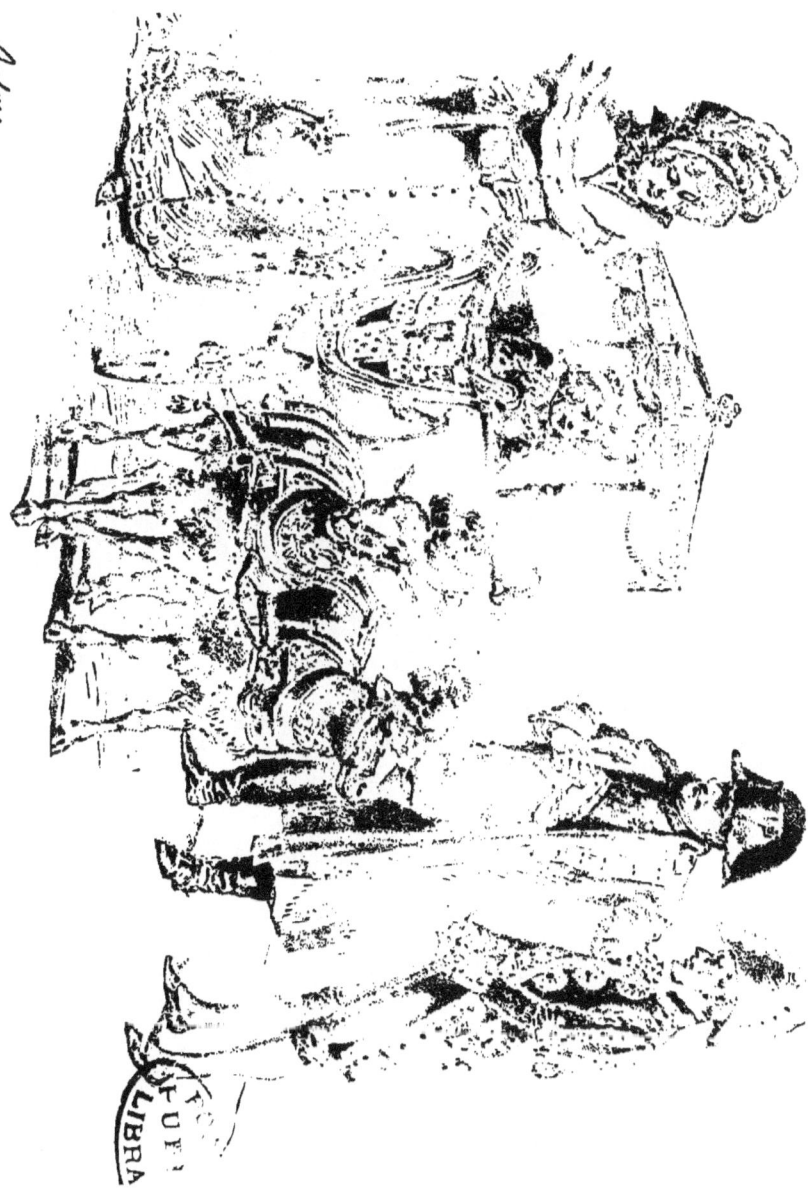

"WHAT CAN YOUR MAJESTY MAKE OF SUCH A DANDY?"

about his uniform. Look, your Majesty," and he pulled Philip toward the little King's carriage, once again in his path, "here's a fellow who thinks more of his rig-out of blue and silver than of France and the Emperor. What can your Majesty make of such a dandy?"

"No, no, Sire; do not say that!" Philip protested, flushed with excitement and pleasure. "But you quite took away my breath with your kindness. I have never dreamed of anything so glorious. And I? Hear me, Sire! I will serve you faithfully."

"I believe you will try, boy Philip—boy no longer, now," the Emperor said kindly. "See that you keep that promise. And remember! It is not for me, but for France, that you labor. For France, the mother of us all."

There were others besides Philip to stand up for France; to shed their blood for France; to conquer, even to die, for the glory of France. But there were others, forced to serve in the great army of three hundred thousand men which as if by magic had risen from the earth at the Emperor's command, who were drilling and marching against their will, and only because of the strong arm of military despotism. There were many who might willingly fight for France, but not for the Emperor. The nation desired peace, the Emperor commanded war; and many followed his eagles against their will.

But let justice be done Napoleon.

"I desire peace," he said at the opening of that battle-spring of 1813. "It is necessary to the world. But I will never make any peace which is not honorable and in conformity with the greatness of my Empire. Our enemies seek the disruption of the Empire. They proclaim universal war. I will conquer them, and bring peace through victory, and give greatness and glory to France."

So, bent on his purpose, the Emperor hastened his preparations for war. The Empress was made Regent of France, to reign in his absence and in his name; and, rank upon rank, the battalions in blue marched toward the Prussian frontier.

On April 15, 1813, Napoleon left St. Cloud to take command of his assembled armies.

Philip was to accompany him. The boy was full of confidence and hope, and so inspired his friends with his bright enthusiasm that even Uncle Fauriel gave the lad his blessing, while Mademoiselle went into ecstasies over his fine appearance, and Corporal Peyrolles was sure "his boy" would return a marshal at least.

At the Tuileries the Emperor joined his staff and his escort of the Guard. There Philip was to meet him, and there, on the morning of that momentous fifteenth of April, the boy ordonnance-officer reported for duty.

Thither had come Pierre and Peyrolles to bid him good-by; and, with Uncle Fauriel as escort, thither came Mademoiselle, bravely smiling through her tears.

The Emperor, in his well-known green uniform and famous cocked hat, appeared in the portal of the palace; the last good-bys were being said; and, now that the time for separation had actually come, Philip and Mademoiselle felt just a trifle awkward.

Even the Emperor had an eye for this little scene, and was on the point of making some characteristic remark, when through the crowd burst Citizen Daunou, his chapeau awry, his white hair all about his ears.

Excited and unceremonious, he cried out as soon as he found the little group, " It fits, Sire! The paper fits. I am an owl no longer. Embrace our Philip, Mademoiselle. It is your right. Bid him God-speed for France! I have made a discovery. You are not Mademoiselle Daunou, as you thought; nor Lucie Marcel, as I thought when I adopted you as my daughter from the home of the sansculotte. Embrace our Philip, Mademoiselle. It is your duty, I say. For you are Mademoiselle Lucie Desnouettes. You are of the best blood of France. And Philip—Philip is your brother!"

CHAPTER XVII

BROTHER AND SISTER

IT was a dramatic method and a tremendous background for springing this surprise. Citizen Daunou, most practical and prosaic of men, could not have arranged things better had he studied to please the Emperor — that lover of startling situations.

To the brother and sister, thus theatrically made known to one another, the revelation was overwhelming. Philip turned white with surprise; Mademoiselle flushed deeply, then paled, as swiftly, and looked with an almost piteous expression upon the man she had always regarded as her father.

Then came the reaction from bewilderment to joy.

"Is it so?" cried Philip.

"What? — it is Philip?" exclaimed Mademoiselle.

And then brother and sister fell into each other's arms. Citizen Daunou's eyes streamed with tears. Uncle Fauriel tossed his chapeau in air. Corporal Peyrolles danced on his one good leg, for joy. Pierre looked on with the satisfaction of one who had been in the secret all along, and actually contemplated one of the old-time hand-springs of his street-boy days. The Emperor walked swiftly to Citizen Daunou and clapped that staid old republican on the back.

"Daunou, is this your work?" he cried. "It is great! You have exceeded my expectations." But Citizen Daunou, just, even in his excitement, said nothing, but waved his hand toward Pierre.

Philip and Mademoiselle, still hand in hand, looked into each other's eyes, laughing and crying in the same moment. For them, the fate of nations, the importance of that historic day, the clouds of war, the peace of Europe, were all forgotten. In all the world there was no one just then but Philip and Lucie. They had found what neither knew, what neither dreamed of.

"I cannot believe it, Philip; can you; can you?" cooed the happy girl.

"My sister; my sister; my sister!" the boy repeated, lingering lovingly on each word. "Tell us, tell us, my father," he said, turning to Citizen Daunou; "what does all this mean? I know it is the truth, but—how did you find it out?"

Then the Emperor broke in: "You shall have time for explanation—you two—you three," he said. "Look you! People say I break up families for my own ambition. They say I sever them in my greed for war. They lie. When France demands her youth for her service I act but as her instrument. But here is no need for haste. *Lieutenant* Desnouettes," he said, emphasizing, to Philip's delight, the rank thus conferred upon him, "I grant you an unlimited leave of absence. Go home with your sister. When I need you, I will summon you to my side. No; no words. I know your willingness to serve me. This is my will. Be happy, my children, for a brief season. I am no ogre to devour a

14

new-found family—though some do deem me so," he added, with a slap, this time, on the fat shoulders of Uncle Fauriel. "Take them home with you, Citizen Daunou. When Philip sees me again, he can tell me all that he has learned. My friend the inspector,"— this to the delighted Pierre,— "I am proud of you. Some day you will yet be a Minister of Police. Adieu, my children!" he said, placing a hand affectionately on the heads of Philip and Mademoiselle. "Until I need you, my Philip, wait here at home. My horse, Constant!" he cried to his valet. Then, vaulting to his saddle, he commanded: "Forward, gentlemen! to Prussia and victory!"

"Long live the Emperor!" rose the shout. The trumpets sounded; the drums rolled; the escort wheeled into line; the green coat and the three-cocked hat disappeared in the distance, as out of the courtyard of the Tuileries and off toward the barriers, the Emperor and his glittering escort galloped through the applauding streets of Paris, off, for the war.

So it came to pass, after all, that Philip did not go to the front with the Emperor, and Citizen Daunou said in a whisper to Pierre:

"Did I not do it well, my friend? I have known this — you know for how many days. But I planned it for a dénoûment; and, my faith! my little plan worked even better than I had hoped." For a staid and sober citizen, the kind old Keeper of the Archives had certainly shown himself a clever and shrewd conspirator.

Still wondering, still hand in hand, the brother and sister walked back to the Street of the Fight. And there, while

all the air was electric with excitement and the presage of
battle, they passed the days in close companionship, careless
of the future, happy in the knowledge and enjoyment of
their new relationship, and making Citizen Daunou tell them,
again and again, the story of how he had unravelled the
mystery and given them, thus, to each other.

The delighted old Keeper never wearied of the tale. He
knew that he had done a good thing and one that would bear
retelling. He told them of their father, the *emigré*—the
man who had died for a principle, almost the last victim of
the tyrants of the Terror. He told them how Nurse Marcel,
the widow of the sansculotte, had, through fear of the con-
sequences, passed off Mademoiselle as her daughter, when
Citizen Daunou had adopted the baby girl into his home, and
how she had lived with her as nurse and companion. He
told how he had found the document that had established
Philip's identity and given him a clue to the discovered relationship. He told of the missing part of the record and
the Emperor's knowledge of the affair; and he gave to Pierre
the inspector all the credit and glory for the discovery that
completed the reading of the riddle.

And then—he had to tell it all over again; while Philip
and Mademoiselle sat, listening, hand in hand, and Pierre,
listening also, nudged Philip excitedly and said, "Not so bad
for 'that pig of a Pierre,' was it now, young Desnonettes?"

Babette, too, Philip's young foster-sister, came in for her
share of the enjoyment, and even Mother Thérèse, sly and
gruff though she was, had to hear the recital and tell her
part of the story, and how the Directory gave her this boy
to bring up; what a good boy he always was (though Philip

wondered when she found that out!), and how she had always said he would be a great man before he died.

So the days passed,—happily, quietly, joyfully. Then came news from the front to increase the general joy. The Emperor had marched to new and glorious victories. At Lützen and at Bautzen he had met and conquered his foes. Triumph was in the air. Peace was surely at hand. All Europe would soon be at the feet of the conqueror. In spite of the Russian campaign the Emperor was again supreme.

Paris went wild with delight. The Empress Regent rode in state to the great church of Notre Dame to hear the Te Deum in praise of the victory; and, when the war was over, the Empress and the King of Rome, it was said, were to be crowned by the Emperor in token of the supremacy and triumph of France.

The battles of Lützen and Bautzen had been stubborn and bloody. Many thousands of brave men had fallen on either side. But what of that? They were victories for France, won by the boys of France—for the fighting-stock of that bloody campaign of 1813 was largely drawn from the youth of France and Germany. Philip had heard with pride how Marshal Ney, "the bravest of the brave," had declared that the boys were better than veterans, and that he could lead them anywhere; and how, at Lützen, the Emperor, in the supreme moment, dashed into the thick of the fight and shouted to the young conscripts who held the center: "My children, I rely upon you to save the Empire! Forward! France is watching you! Learn how to die for her!" And they did. For, with ringing shouts of "Long live the Emperor!" the boys then charged the Prussians, and, with the bayonet's point, turned the tide of battle and won the day for France.

This was most inspiriting. Already, notwithstanding the happy days with his new-found sister, Philip felt himself growing uneasy and wishing for the call to action. It came at last. One day an order was delivered to him bearing the imperial seal:

> Lieutenant Philip Desnouettes, of the Officers of Ordonnance, is directed to accompany the Empress to Mayence and report for duty to the Emperor in person.

An armistice had been declared. Lützen and Bautzen had called for a truce in the war; overtures for peace were made by Austria, a neutral power, and agreed to by France on the one side and by the allied powers of Russia, Prussia, and Sweden on the other. And, in July, Napoleon, resting from battle, requested his Empress to join him for a few days at Mayence; for the armistice declared a cessation of hostilities until the tenth of August following.

"I go to join the Emperor," Philip announced joyfully to his sister and his good friends in the Street of the Fight. "But, alas! I am destined never to see service in the field. We shall have peace, and the Emperor will be the master of Europe."

"I hope so, my son," Citizen Daunou said; "but I do not believe it. The enemies of France are too many and too determined. They will fight to the death and crush us by numbers. This conflict is not like those that have gone before. Our foemen have learned the art of war from the

Emperor. They will turn their knowledge to fatal account. This armistice is but the prelude to a yet more bloody fight, and a defeat will be our death-blow. Oh, that the Emperor would see his opportunity! France asks for peace; the world asks for it. By it the Emperor might confound his enemies and bring about results more glorious than the most victorious war. But he will not. See, Philip! Already the report is abroad that on the summit of the Alps Napoleon is to erect a monument on which will be inscribed: 'Napoleon to the French People, in memory of its noble efforts against the coalition of 1813.' To-day the Emperor is great; he is victorious. How much greater, how much more the victor would he be, if he would sign a treaty of peace, giving up the needless provinces he has conquered, and inscribe upon that treaty the words: 'These are the sacrifices to peace made by Napoleon for the welfare of the people of France.' But he will not do it, my son. He will not do it."

Philip could not agree with his old friend. What young fellow, living in an atmosphere of victory, would believe that there was such a thing as a giving that was gaining!

He bade his dear ones adieu, reported for duty as one of the cortége of the Empress, and in high spirits set out to join the Emperor, then resting at Mayence.

They rode from St. Cloud on the twenty-third of July, stopping on the way at Châlons and at Metz, and on the twenty-sixth reached Mayence. And there Philip again saw the Emperor.

"So, my noble young lieutenant of ordonnance," cried Napoleon, pulling Philip's ear by way of friendly greeting, "you are ready for duty, eh? And how is the pretty sister in Paris? It was an excellent bit of acting, that. Do you know, my Philip, I half suspect good Citizen Daunou of springing it upon us for a purpose. He is a shrewd old schemer, I fear—that Daunou—for all his quiet ways as a browser among dusty documents. But it gave you a pleasure —you and Mademoiselle, your sister. Now, see what you can do to make her proud of her relationship. You will. Be but less heedless than of old, and more the man you are now big enough to be."

Festivities made brilliant the brief visit of the Empress to Mayence. Princes and potentates thronged the audience chamber. Fêtes and illuminations, reviews and receptions, balls and banquets, crowded each other for ten days, and the old Rhenish city was full of stir and splendor.

But, beneath all this, lay anxiety. The world wished for peace; yet the world would know, all too well, the unbending will of the Emperor.

One day Philip received a shock. After a grand dinner given by the Emperor to his titled tributaries, the boy accompanied Napoleon for a sail on the Rhine. The shores of the historic river lay picturesque and pleasant under a summer sun, and the Emperor, passing the castle of Biberich, stood with one foot on the gunwale of the boat, studying the shore through his field-glass.

As the Emperor leaned dangerously over the edge, Philip heard the prefect of Mayence—a stout old republican of the Directory days—say in an undertone to his neighbor, the governor of Berg: "Look there! What an opportunity! The fate of the world hangs on a single kick!"

"In heaven's name, hush!" whispered the terrified governor.

"Bah! do not fret," returned the old prefect: "resolute men are rare."

Philip glanced at the old republican in ill-concealed terror. Kick the Emperor overboard! Would he dare do this? Why, it was worse than Uncle Fauriel.

But the old prefect turned from temptation with a sigh. "Ah, my friend," he said to the trembling governor, "let me tell you, we shall all of us lament with tears of blood that this boat-trip was not the Corsican's last."

Philip mused over this startling incident. It was, indeed, the undercurrent of talk that he had heard far too often of late. His loyalty to the Emperor made him nervous and angry, and he wondered whether it were not his duty to report it all. Then he reassured himself with the thought: "The Emperor will have his way, and all these traitorous grumblers will humbly eat their words and give him greater glory than ever."

The Emperor did have his way. He refused to listen to the appeals of Austria and the demands of Russia. Not an inch of French conquest would he resign. The enemies of France should sue to him as to a victor. He would never be a suppliant.

The tenth of August came. Hostilities were resumed. Austria broke her pledges and joined the enemies of France; and under the walls of Dresden, Napoleon, with less than a hundred thousand men, hurled himself against the allied powers of Europe, nearly two hundred thousand strong.

There Philip first "smelled gunpowder." There he received his "baptism of fire." There for the first time he heard the thunder of hostile cannon, the clash of opposing

"THE EYE OF THE EMPEROR, HE FELT, WAS UPON HIM."

steel, the shrill neigh of the war-horse, the hoarse shouts of command, the mingling cries of combatants, the swelling cheer of the victor, the sullen growl of the vanquished, the backward note of retreat, the forward yell of pursuit, the sharp scream of the wounded, the muffled groan of the dying, and all the pomp and pain, all the glory and misery of that legalized murder that men call war.

He heard all, he saw all, he was a part of all. At first, kept busy in writing and despatching orders rapidly dictated by the Emperor—that master of the art of war, whose eye seemed everywhere, whose ear heard everything—Philip paid but little attention to the details of the conflict. Then, despatched on some imperative mission, he came face to face with death—looked at it, paled before it, trembled before it, braced himself before it, and at last, all on fire with excitement, desire, and duty, hardened himself in the midst of it, and became as reckless, as daring, as heedless and as unconcerned as any of the thousands of young conscripts who made up the victorious army of Napoleon that brilliant day of struggle and achievement beneath the walls of Dresden.

Three times his duty carried him into the thick of the fight, amidst flying bullets, falling fighters, the rush of battalions and the clash of steel. The eye of the Emperor, he felt, was upon him—that Emperor who, braving death a hundred times, saw this weak spot, reckoned on that movement, hurled his squadrons against this wall of men, massed his infantry for a charge upon that yielding break, and fighting, sword in hand, like any sub-lieutenant in the ranks, unmindful of the torrents of driving rain, heedless of the oceans of clogging mud, cried: "Forward, my children! again! again! I cannot be beaten!" and added to his laurels as a conqueror the masterly victory of Dresden.

Philip was roused; he was electrified; he grew full of the fury of the battle. He galloped this way and that, commanding, crying, cheering, carried away with excitement. And when he rode with the hussars, pursuing the routed Russians, he saw the only enemy that remained to face the victorious Frenchmen—a great, alert, watchful-eyed Danish hound, searching for his master.

Philip whistled cheerily, and the dog came at the call. Then it bristled with growl and bark, as this boy it did not know leaned from his saddle to pet and capture it. The chase slackened; the bugles sounded the recall; and when, the battle over, the enemy flying, the victory won, Philip rode back to the French lines, he brought with him as the only trophy of his valor a single prisoner—this dog.

He glanced at the hound's gleaming collar. Upon it he read: *I am General Moreau's dog.*

"Moreau? Moreau?" he queried. "It is a French name." Can it be that renegade?

"Ha! Moreau the deserter! Moreau the renegade! Moreau the traitor! Kill the dog!" cried the soldiers; for the presence of Moreau, once the greatest of French fighters,—Moreau, the victor of Hohenlinden—as a leader in the ranks of the enemy, infuriated and enraged the army.

"Hands off! the dog is my prisoner!" Philip cried.

The soldiers yielded to the young lieutenant with a laugh. And when Philip rode through the gates of Dresden, he carried with him this captured pet of Napoleon's old-time comrade and rival—now dying among the enemies of France.

CHAPTER XVIII

"THE CLAWS OF THE CORSICAN"

PHILIP dismounted, and, still followed by his prisoner, entered the palace of the Saxon kings, in which the Emperor had his headquarters.

There he found Napoleon — wet, bedraggled, tired, but triumphant — with the brim of his cocked hat hanging in ruin upon his shoulder, and the famous gray overcoat black with mud. The Emperor had been three days without rest, and twelve hours in the pouring rain. But he had won the fight; he had sent the enemy flying across the Saxon borders, and satisfaction and delight shone upon his face.

"Ah, ha! my ordonnance boy," he cried. "You are there, eh? And how is it with you? You have worked hard; you have worked faithfully. He who writes and rides may be as brave as he who carries the eagles or waves the sword. I am proud of you, young Desnouettes."

Praise is a wonderful medicine. It is rest for tired bones; it is balm for smarting wounds; it is even comfort in dying. To a boy who feels that he really has done his duty, it is especially sweet to hear the words, "Well done!" And praise from Napoleon was both a reward and an inspiration.

Philip grasped the Emperor's extended hand, and kissed it in acknowledgment. "Sire," he said, "you can never be beaten! I would not have missed this day for all the palaces in Paris."

Napoleon smiled again. Then he spied the hound and asked, "Ah, that dog? Is it Moreau's, as I have heard?"

"So says his collar, Sire," Philip replied. "I took him prisoner in a cottage at Racknitz."

"Racknitz!" exclaimed the Emperor. "But that was where I trained the guns upon the Russian staff. Philip, Philip! it may have been I who killed the renegade! Poor Moreau!" said Napoleon, passing his hand over his brow, "to die a traitor because he hated 'that rascal Bonaparte,' as he called me! I honored him once, though he was ever jealous of me. France! I have avenged you of a degenerate son. Well; all goes finely. Rest yourself, Lieutenant Desnouettes, and to-morrow prepare to ride with me—very early, remember—to our camp at Pirna. We must follow fast on the runaways and smother them in the hills. And then — on to Berlin!"

To the great camp at Pirna—ten miles southeast of Dresden—Philip rode with the Emperor, and was at once busied in writing orders directing the pursuit of the demoralized allies.

Suddenly, in the midst of an order to General Vandamme, who was to head off the retreat near Kulm, a hundred miles to the north, the Emperor gave a sharp cry, clapped a hand over his lowest waistcoat buttons, and doubled up completely, unable to think or act.

Napoleon had the stomach-ache.

You laugh at this; but, let me tell you, there is nothing so demoralizing as pain. Headache and indigestion have wrecked more than one great cause. Men who can command armies have surrendered to the toothache. Napoleon was never victorious on the sea, because he was always too seasick to command in person. Washington bore pain without flinching, and set the government of the new United States on its feet, while nearly dying from a boil on his leg; Napoleon could not endure pain, and lost his crown through a stomach-ache. For the cramp that caught him that day at Pirna kept him from pursuing his routed foes, and, with that failure to act, began the conqueror's downfall.

At all events, he gave up his plan of conducting the pursuit in person. He returned to Dresden. Disaster fell upon his generals whenever they fought without him. Oudinot was beaten at Grossbeeren; Macdonald was overthrown at Katzbach; Vandamme was captured at Kulm; Ney was routed at Dennewitz. The Allies turned back; with fresh troops swelling their recovering ranks, they drew about the man they had sworn to destroy.

His vassals forsook him; his tributaries deserted him. France was left alone; and, yielding to the advice of his marshals rather than following his own wise judgment, Napoleon gave up his plan of marching upon Berlin. His enemies drew about him; they inclosed him in a ring of steel; and on the sixteenth of October, in that year of 1813, the Emperor stood at bay under the walls of quaint old Leipsic — a handful against a host

That bloodiest battle of modern times has been called the Battle of the Nations. It was France against all Europe. For three days it raged. One hundred and ten thousand men were killed or wounded. Then the Saxons in the ranks of France went over in a body to the enemy. Retreat was a necessity. Napoleon was beaten. But he would not admit it. Neither would Philip. The boy was worked nearly to death. He rode, he wrote, he ran; he scurried about amid flying bullets, looked almost down the throats of belching cannon, got himself entangled in moving masses of infantry, and dodged many a sweeping cavalry charge. He was growing heedless of danger; he was becoming used to war.

He was angry to see that, instead of pursuing, the French were really in retreat. But Philip did not call it a retreat; he spoke of it as "a backward movement." He scowled with rage as he railed at the "treacherous Saxons"; and, when the crowning disaster came—the blowing-up of the bridge over the Elster, which cut off the French rear-guard, the wagon-train, and the wounded—Philip echoed the Emperor, and declared that it was disaster and not defeat that took away the glory from the great victory of Leipsic—the "victory" that all the world now knows to have been a most disastrous defeat.

Then came the fight at Hanau, the last gleam of sunshine through the gathering clouds—for Napoleon turned it into a success—and, on the first day of November, Philip was despatched to Paris as the herald of victory, carrying to the Empress Regent the twenty hostile standards captured at Leipsic and Hanau.

His coming cheered people greatly, for it showed them that the Emperor was victorious; and Philip was praised and petted on every hand.

From the palace, as soon as his duties were over, Philip

"HE SHOWED HER WHERE A TATAR ARROW HAD TORN AN UGLY HOLE."

flew to the Street of the Fight, the great hound stalking at his heels.

"Mademoiselle my sister," he said, after the glad greeting was over, "I bring you the first captive of my bow and spear. I lay my trophy at your feet. Down, 'Marshal!' Crouch!" and the big Dane, trained by his captor for this very act of homage, first hung his head, as if in acknowledgment of his defeat, and then crouched, a suppliant, at the feet of the delighted girl.

"O Philip!—for me? How lovely! What a beauty! See, Nurse, I shall not need you longer as a chaperone. Here is my protector," and she rested her little hand on the great dog's head. "But, Philip, did you really fight with bow and spear? They tell us the Cossacks do."

Philip laughed with the superior air of a veteran. "Well, *we* do not, Mademoiselle," he replied. "But the Tatars and Bashkirs do. Pestiferous little Russian wasps! I caught one of their arrows through my chapeau. See!" and, drawing his hat from beneath his arm, he showed where a Tatar arrow had torn an ugly hole. "My best one, too," he added, gazing on it ruefully; while Mademoiselle regarded the rent with awe, and then cried:

"Oh, but suppose it had not gone so high, my Philip! Oh, dear!" and with a little shriek she transferred her caressing hand from the great Dane's neck to her brother's curly head.

Soon his other friends gathered in welcome and admiration, and the boy's rattling chatter almost dispelled the gloom he noted on all their faces. For despite the elation over the pretended victories, Paris was downcast and anxious.

"A fine mess your Corsican is getting us into, young Desnouettes!" blurted out Uncle Fauriel. "Why, before we know it, we shall have the Allies storming into Paris itself. And what then?"

"Never!" cried Philip, hotly. "Paris will never be occupied by the foes of France while the Emperor lives. I tell you he is master!"

"How can he be, my Philip, with half a million men crowding him against a wall?" Citizen Daunou said, sadly. "I acknowledge the Emperor's greatness. I know his mighty will. He will not give up without a blow. The hour for great souls is that when everything is lost. But even his valor cannot withstand a host. We have no men left to fight for him. Let him make peace, or his empire is doomed."

"I know his valor, too," said Uncle Fauriel. "But your Emperor is no Frenchman. He is a Corsican. And the Corsican, like the cat, persists in spitting, and squirming, and scratching, even when one holds him by the nape of the neck. Europe holds your Emperor thus. But let Europe beware. Your Emperor at bay is but a cat in a corner. You shall yet see the claws of the Corsican."

Within a few days after Philip's arrival the Emperor himself returned to Paris. He came unannounced. He came almost in disgrace. Again he had lost an army for France. But pride was in his heart and determination in his eye.

"Peace?" he cried. "Who talks of peace with the enemy at our gates? We must fight once more. We must fight desperately, and, when we have conquered, then we will talk of peace. I desire peace, but it must be solid and honorable. France depends upon me. I am a man who may be killed, but never will be insulted. The French will be worthy of themselves and me."

With that he set about to raise a new army for the defense of France. "In three months we shall have peace," he said. The enemy will be driven out, or I shall be dead. My soldiers and I have not forgotten our trade, and those who dared profane our frontier shall soon repent of having stepped foot on French soil."

Already "the Corsican," as Uncle Fauriel had declared, was sharpening his "claws."

The foot of the foeman was on French soil. The Allies crossed the Rhine; they had invaded France. The nation, accustomed only to attack, was unprepared to defend; Paris was without fortifications; the fighting material the Emperor demanded was not easy to procure. Twenty years of war had well-nigh drained France of men.

But the Emperor was imperative. "Give me soldiers!" he said. Men-soldiers! I cannot fight your battles with children. Our boys of the Young Guard fought nobly at Dresden and Leipsic; nothing can exceed their courage. But in the struggle before us, if I am to conquer, I must have men, men, men!"

The men came, and the boys as well. Though all France cried for peace; though Paris wailed, "This insatiate one wishes to sacrifice all our children to his wild ambition"; and though this wail was echoed in every town and village of the Empire, still the Senate, accustomed to obey the Emperor, voted both the men and the money he demanded; and in January, 1814, France had collected nearly three hundred thousand men with which to oppose an invading force of almost a million.

Philip was speedily summoned to join the Emperor. His duties had permitted him frequent glimpses of that charming home-life that was one phase of this strange man's character, when he would play like a child with his boy, the little King of Rome; and Philip, too, was with the Emperor that sad and eventful January day when Napoleon committed to the care of the Home Guard of Paris his wife and child, and left to face his foes. "Gentlemen," he said to the officers of this Home Guard, "France is invaded. I place myself at the head of my army, and with the help of God and the valor of my troops I shall drive the enemy beyond the frontiers." Then, giving one hand to the Empress and one to the little King, he presented them to the Guards: "To you, gentlemen," he said, "I confide the protection of my wife and my son, on whom so many hopes rest. I intrust them to you; I intrust them to the affectionate care of my faithful city of Paris."

The Guards wept; the Guards swore fealty; the Guards shouted: "Long live the Emperor!" Then he was gone; and, straightway, with all the wariness and all the ferocity of a tiger, he sprang at the throat of his foe.

It was a death grapple, desperate, brilliant, dramatic. It was a struggle magnificent in its intensity, masterly in its conception, wonderful in its devices. It is too little known in history, overshadowed by the glory of Austerlitz, the disaster of Moscow, the carnage of Leipsic, the tragedy of Waterloo. It was the conqueror at bay.

Ten times, in that short campaign, did Napoleon face and overthrow his hunters. All his strategy, all his daring, all his brilliant methods were brought into play; and, each time, the invaders reeled back, defeated, bleeding, and broken. The "claws of the Corsican" struck swiftly and sank deep.

Twice was Philip sent to Paris with flags as trophies and prisoners as signs of triumph. Then, one March afternoon, the Emperor summoned him in haste.

"Lieutenant Desnouettes," he said, "I intrust you with this letter to the Empress. Be wary and be vigilant. Guard it with your life. Deliver it only into the Empress's own hands. It is because I know your courage and your loyalty that I repose this trust in you. Ride, for life or death!"

Philip sprang to his saddle and galloped toward Paris.

The sun was nearly set as he rode out of the little hamlet of St.-Dizier (where Napoleon, next day, was to win his last victory) and headed for Paris. The night favored the rider; for, with the continual changing of positions, one was always in danger, and darkness was a convenient cloak. If but he could escape the enemy's outposts or their foraging parties, his way was clear.

So he rode on with speed. From St.-Dizier to Perthe and Villotte and Vitry-on-the-Marne he rode; and, crossing the river, spurred on to Cosle and Connantray and La Fère-Champenoise, where, one to ten, the French had fought the invaders, and Pacthod's guards had proven themselves heroes. Soon he galloped into Sézanne. Thus far all was well. But, as he rode from Sézanne, he hesitated. The road to Coulommiers was the most direct; but he knew the upper road better, where, from Montmirail, the road led westward to Meaux.

He decided for the upper road, and there was his mistake.

For, as he saw the lights of Montmirail shining across the narrow Little Morin, and looked for the white streak that meant the road to Meaux, he spied, ahead, a moving blur, magnified by the darkness into an uncertain but threatening mass. He tried to force his horse from the road and into the bordering fields, although he knew that thus he would miss the bridge across the Little Morin and have to swim for it.

In the gloom of the night his horse, like a sensible beast, refused to leave the road or jump the low wall that flanked the roadway.

The moving mass came on with shout and swing. Philip had been seen. The challenge rang sharply out, but Philip held his peace, refusing a reply. Then bullets whistled by him, and the boy, thinking safety lay only in his own legs, dismounted and let his horse go free.

With the "Hurra!" that he now knew so well as the Cossack war-cry, his foemen swooped upon the riderless horse; but, seeing through the boy's plan, dashed across the bridge, and stretched themselves in a crescent from wall to wall.

Then Philip sought to climb the wall, and escape across the fields to the bank of the stream. But he was stiff with riding, and, in the darkness, his footing was insecure. He slipped and fell almost beneath the hoofs of the oncoming horse.

Again he heard the guttural call, the terrible Cossack "Hurra!" Then something pounced upon him in the dark, before he could free his pistol-hand or draw his sword. Eager hands felt for and grabbed him. He squirmed and dodged and wriggled and kicked, but all to no purpose.

The next instant he was lifted to his feet; a light was flashed full upon him; fierce faces encircled him; words he did not understand shot from bearded and swarthy lips. He could neither defend nor assail. He could not even die, as he had sworn he would, if cornered. Philip was a prisoner in the hands of the Cossacks.

PHILIP TAKEN PRISONER BY THE COSSACKS.

CHAPTER XIX

HOW THE SCHOOLBOYS FOUGHT AT PARIS

PHILIP struggled desperately in the hands of his captors, but to no avail. He was speedily secured and conducted to headquarters, only to find—just see how curiously things come around!—that he had fallen into the hands of the Cossacks of Czernicheff's command—that Russian about whom Philip the page got into trouble by calling the Czar's envoy "Catch-a-sneezy the spy," the day when, in the Hall of the Marshals, he had angered the Russian ambassador.

Philip felt a little uncertain when he discovered this. He recalled the stories of Russian vengeance he had so often heard, and expected the worst. But there was no especial danger. Czernicheff did not recognize in this bedraggled young courier the spruce palace page of the days of magnificence. He saw that it was a bearer of despatches his Cossacks had captured, and he hurried the prisoner on to Marshal Blücher's headquarters for examination.

Old "Marshal Forward," as Blücher had been nicknamed because of his continual cry of "Forward to Paris!" questioned his prisoner sharply as to the mission on which he rode; but Philip answered never a word. .

"Thunder and lightning! Has the boy no tongue? Search him!" Blücher cried hotly.

And they did search him, more thoroughly than gently. Philip was punched and pummeled and pinched and fingered and finally stripped, in this eager search for the letter he was supposed to be carrying to court. At last it was ripped out from the secret pocket in the boy's crimson vest, and with a hurrah! of discovery handed to the old Prussian leader, who, meanwhile, had stood by, watching the proceedings, pulling his long mustache, and growling in choicest German at the boy's obstinacy.

Blücher tore open the letter and read it hastily. "So! for the Empress, is it? And not in cipher," he cried. "That is good!—As I thought!" he exclaimed. "The Corsican is in sore straits, and—what!—means to march to the east? Ha! he would strike at our rear, would he? and draw us back to the Rhine? We shall see; we shall see. It is but a desperate man's last device. Yes, this proves it—this last line here—what is it? 'This step saves me or ruins me.' So! Quick! copy it—copy it, Rudolph!" he cried, throwing the letter into the hands of one of his staff secretaries. "The commander-in-chief shall read it and see that my advice was best. Now he shall come to my way of thinking."

The commander-in-chief of the allied armies—that same Prince Schwarzenberg at whose famous and fatal ball Philip had first met Mademoiselle—evidently did speedily come to Blücher's way of thinking. For, before two days had passed, the Allies were racing for Paris, each division anxious to be the first to attack the imperiled and helpless capital; while Napoleon's shrewd, though desperate move to draw back the enemy was thwarted, because he had been in too much of a hurry, and had not written in cipher his letter to the Empress.

PHILIP BEFORE MARSHAL BLÜCHER. THE LETTER IS FOUND.

But before this came about, Philip was released; and, escorted to the French outpost at Meaux, was sent on to Paris as bearer of the letter, which the enemy had already read and profited by.

He felt small enough as he rode dejectedly from Meaux, through the forest and village of Bondy, and along the Canal of Ourcq. As he entered the city by the temple-like gate at the Villette barrier, he felt almost tempted to fling himself into the broad basin into which the canal flows. He had been a miserable failure. He had promised to defend his mission with his life; and here he was, a cat's-paw for the enemy, bearing the letter, to be sure, but only after it had been taken from him and turned to such terrible account. What would the Emperor say? What would be the end of it all?

With a shrug of the shoulders—his convenient French way of saying, "Well, I can't help it!" he threw off the unpleasant thought, and said to himself, "After all, it is as the Emperor himself says in such cases—the fortune of war! I did my best." And then he rode down the Street of the Suburb of St. Martin and on to the Tuileries.

Philip sought the Empress and gave her the letter and the truth. The girl looked troubled—after all, she was but a girl.

"How careless!" she exclaimed. "Both you and the Emperor! How could you be thus caught, young Desnouettes? And why—oh, why, did the Emperor write, when he has always sent his other letters in a cipher the enemy cannot read? How dreadful! Listen: 'This step saves me or ruins me,' he says. I see only ruin now. What shall I do? whom can I trust? who will advise?"

"Madame, stay!" cried Philip, impulsively, dropping upon his knee. "Stay, and save Paris. The Home Guard swore to protect you and the little King. Stay; and all Paris will die in defending you."

"Monsieur the lieutenant, for all your boasting, you are but a fool," returned the young Empress, sharply, snatching away her robe from the touch of the appealing boy. "Paris! You do not know the town. It would not turn a finger to save the daughter of Austria. Paris! It is like the champagne it loves too well — all fizz to-day, all dead to-morrow. It is full of traitors and turncoats — men who will cry, 'Long live the Emperor!' in the morning, and 'Down with Bonaparte!' at night. And the Emperor? He bids me go. He declares he had rather see his son in the Seine than in the hands of the Allies. Did I come to Paris but for this? Am I to be like my grand-aunt, poor Marie Antoinette, whom your dear Paris murdered? Boy, boy — you are no better than the others! No one can advise me. Everything is crumbling. We are lost!"

Was there no hope? Philip, roused to frenzy over the way things were going, hurried to the Street of the Fight. It was as quiet there as ever — Mademoiselle at her tasks, Citizen Dannou lost in his dusty documents of by-gone days, Nurse Marcel stolidly industrious.

They greeted Philip with joy. They exclaimed in surprise at his torn and discolored uniform. "You look tired and worried, my Philip. What have you been going through?" Mademoiselle asked.

Philip told his story of the mission and the capture. He begged them to do something.

HOW THE SCHOOLBOYS FOUGHT AT PARIS

"Paris is in danger — in danger!" he cried to Citizen Daunou. "Cannot you, my father, do something? Cannot we rouse men to its defence?"

"And wherefore, my Philip? What may we hope to do?" Citizen Daunou said. "We are but drinking the cup I promised you months ago. You see now the Emperor's greatest mistake. He has given grand fortifications, arsenals, troops, all necessary defenses, to his distant cities — to Dantzic, to Hamburg, to Flushing, to Venice. But to Paris — nothing! 'Paris could never be invaded! No foeman's foot could ever press the sacred soil of France!' Oh, no! But to-day that foot is here — here at the very gates of Paris. And what have we to protect us? Nothing, Philip; nothing — not even the Emperor! Here is no armament; here are no muskets, no cannon, no fortifications. And for defenders — not thirty thousand men to drive back half a million! And the Emperor is not here!"

"But he will be here," cried Philip, bravely. "He will be here, and then let the Cossacks tremble! The Emperor alone is worth half a million men."

"If he were here, yes," replied Citizen Daunou. "But he is not here; and through the ranks of the enemy even he cannot break to save us. He is not here, and at the palace are only weaklings and traitors. The Empress is but a child — and a foreigner. Her father leads our foes. King Joseph is timid and dares not take a step for fear of his brother the Emperor. The War Minister is an incompetent; the Police Minister is an imbecile; the Arch-Chancellor is an old grandfather; Prince Talleyrand is a traitor. They will leave us, you will see. They will leave us, and Paris will fall."

The old republican was right. Next day the Empress and her council fled from Paris—the only one of them with spunk enough to stay being the three-year-old King of Rome, who cried and kicked, and refused to leave — and who never saw Paris again.

And, even as the Court fled, the watchers could see from the heights about the city, and from the towers of Notre Dame, the head of the Russian column winding out of the Bondy woods, leading the advance of that army of invasion that drew steadily toward the capital — Paris, beautiful Paris, which for centuries had not seen the smoke of hostile camp-fires, nor the gleam of hostile steel, and yet which its own citizens seemed to have neither the spirit nor the patriotism to defend.

However, the next morning,— the thirtieth of March, 1814,— when at day-break the booming of the Russian cannon told that the attack had begun, there were those who rushed to the aid of the men outside the barriers, already drawn up in line of battle. Militiamen with the loaf of bread that must be their dinner sticking on their bayonet points; workingmen carrying pistols or the rusty pike that was a relic of their fathers' valor in the days of the Sansculotte; citizens carrying fowling-pieces as if they were bound on a bird-hunt, these all ran through the streets crying "To arms!" and headed for the barriers.

In line of battle beyond the barriers, extending in a semicircle about the eastern side of the city, from the Seine on the south to the gate of Clichy on the north, were ranged the real defenders—twelve thousand soldiers of the grand army under the Marshals Marmont and Mortie, a few thousand Home Guards, a few thousand raw recruits drawn from their barracks, veterans from the Soldiers' Home, and the schoolboys of the military and scientific schools of Paris.

It was these last who bore the brunt of the battle. Philip felt a thrill of pride as he saw among the defenders of the city he loved the boys of his old school at Alfort, and the Polytechnic boys. He waved his hat excitedly as he galloped past them, and cried again and again: "Stick to your guns, fellows! We boys will do it yet!"

Philip knew that, rightly, he should have broken through the lines and gone to report to the Emperor. But how could he? There was to be a battle. Could he leave when every fighting-man was needed—while hostile cannon were playing against his city, his friends, his school-fellows? He elected to stay, and, full of ardor and determination, he reported to Marshal Marmont as a special aide, and galloped from point to point, from barrier to barrier, bearing messages, and striking a blow for Paris whenever he had the chance.

For ten hours the battle raged. Here, the shattered ranks of the Sixth Corps—heroes of sixty-seven battles within the last ninety days—stood stoutly against the foemen, whom, again and again, they had seen break and run before their charges; there, the old soldiers, whose fighting days were over, once more leveled their muskets against the foes of France. The conscripts, yet new to war, fought with the dash of veterans; and in the woods of Romainville, by the bridge of Charenton, on the heights of Montmartre, and at the Clichy gate, the boys of the Paris schools served the guns like trained artillerists, and fought from tree to tree like seasoned frontiersmen in American forests. They were determined to do or die for France.

Even valor may be overborne by numbers.

Again and again were the Allies driven back. Again and again, with ever-increasing numbers, did they return to the assault. Men and boys were falling everywhere. The battle of Paris was one of the most stubborn and one of the most hopeless of all the conflicts of that hopeless campaign of 1814. If but Napoleon had been there, that last of the battles might have proved a victory.

Philip had rallied with the boys of the Young Guard as they drove the Prussians back to the suburbs of Pantin and St. Gervais; he slashed and shot in the wood of Romainville; and, spurring in the advance, cheered on his schoolfellows of Alfort as the cavalry class charged straight upon the Russian grenadiers at the bridge of Charenton. When, flanked and outnumbered, the boys crossed the Seine and made a desperate stand on the Beauregard slope, Philip was with them to cheer and wave his sword as their brave commander urged them to stand firm, and shouted, "At them again, boys! Behind you is Paris; before you is the foe!"

Galloping to the north with a message for the dauntless Marshal Mortier, he joined in the fight before the Barrier of the Throne, where stood the three hundred Polytechnic boys, one of whom, when taken prisoner, cheekily demanded of the Russian general a letter of recommendation to Siberia in order that he might teach mathematics there!

Behind their battery, holding their crazy fort, the Polytechnic boys stood like a wall. Philip cheered his old schoolfellows until he was hoarse as, again and again, they drove back the Russian cavalry charges; and, when they were outnumbered, and their battery was taken, he galloped

CORPORAL PEYROLLES AND THE POLYTECHNIC BOYS FIGHTING IN THE DEFENSE OF PARIS.

amid their mass, as with an irresistible rush they swooped upon their assailants, recaptured, and dragged off their precious guns.

He waved his shako wildly, as, dashing past the hillock of Chaumont, he saw at the guns, with a schoolboy on one side and a veteran on the other, dear old one-legged Peyrolles, who, begrimed with powder-smoke, stopped just an instant while sighting his unerring piece, to wave his hand to Philip and shout, " Eh, there, my Philip! Long live the Emperor!"

And, as he reached the barriers at the Clichy gate, where brave old Marshal Moncey made the last desperate stand behind the hastily-made barricades which soldiers, students, citizens, women, and children had helped to build, Philip, as he sprang from his reeking horse, leaped almost into the arms of a fat man who, blackened with powder, and with the perspiration streaming from every pore, was reloading an old fowling-piece, now hot from rapid firing.

"What! Uncle Fauriel?" cried Philip. "You here?"

"And why not?" Uncle Fauriel answered, ramming home another charge. "Where is the Corsican?"

"Coming, coming, if we will but wait," Philip answered, with a wail of anxious fear. "Don't let us give in; I know he will come."

"Bah!" said Uncle Fauriel. "And why is he not here now, boy?— making peaceable fellows like us good citizens look after his business!" he grumbled.

"But why you?" queried Philip.

"Why me, boy?" cried Uncle Fauriel, deliberately sighting his piece toward the Russian ranks; " why not, then? If the Corsican is beaten the White Cockade comes in; and, as between Bonaparte and the Bourbons, give me the Corsican. I did not build up the Republic, my Philip, to let the Empire, which is the child of the Republic, give in to the aristocrats we kicked out in '93. What is that you say— the fight is over? the foreigners have whipped us? Never! Down with the Allies! Down with the Royalists!"—here he fired again—" Long live the Emperor!"

There came a flash of flame from the Russian guns, and Uncle Fauriel staggered, reeled, and fell back—dead.

Even as he fell, the white flag fluttered out; the guns of assailants and defenders were silent; the battle was over; Paris had surrendered. And Philip, gazing on the face of his old friend, gave to it both a smile and a tear.

"Dear Uncle Fauriel!" he cried. "Victor though vanquished! Dying for the man whose empire he hated; fighting for the cause he detested only less than the cause he fought against; a loyal son of France—his last words a wish for the man he had all his life resisted; his last thought a prayer for the Corsican! Dear Uncle Fauriel!"

CHAPTER XX

THE FALL OF THE TRICOLOR

BESIEGERS and besieged fell back from their positions. The wounded were borne off; the dead were removed; and Philip, desperate over the defeat, broken-hearted at the death of his old friend, hurried to the Street of the Fight to tell the sad story.

Mademoiselle mingled her tears with those of her brother as he told of Uncle Fauriel's death. But Citizen Daunou smiled sadly and said, "After all, my children, it was the taking-off that best suited that stanch old Convention-man. One half his talk was bluster, but the other half was real patriotism. As against Napoleon the Corsican, Uncle Fauriel was ever hot and bitter; but Bonaparte, the hope of the Directory, as against the Bourbons whom that Directory drove from France, was a cause which, when the hour came, our dear old patriot was ready to defend with his blood. He was right in his fears; the Bourbons will come in again; and I should never have been able to restrain Uncle Fauriel's fierce hatred against the cause they represent. He would ever have been in trouble. Better for him the glorious death he met, there at the Clichy gate, than to be the tool of political plotters and the dupe of foolish conspirators. In this world, my children, it is better to be loyal than uncertain. Trust me, our France, though defeated now, will never forget such valiant sons of France as Uncle Fauriel."

And, to-day, the striking and beautiful monument which Paris has raised in memory of those brave citizen-soldiers who fell at the Clichy gate attests the truth of Citizen Daunou's prophecy.

But, in life, one must think of the living; and Philip felt, now that his duty as a defender was done, that his place was at the side of his Emperor.

At two o'clock on the morning of March thirty-first, the authorities in command at Paris signed the capitulation, and the tricolored banner came down from its staff on the Tuileries. Before daybreak Philip was far from Paris, galloping along the road by which, according to the latest reports, the Emperor was hurrying to the relief of his capital.

As the dusk was just turning to dawn, Philip rode into the little hamlet of Fromenteau, some twelve miles from Paris; and, in the dim morning light, he saw before him a well-known figure walking in the direction of the fallen city.

He understood at once. The Emperor had received the news of the defeat and the surrender, and, fretting at every delay, without waiting for horse or carriage, was starting to walk toward Paris, a dozen miles away. For once, even his coolness had yielded to impatience. Almost on his heels hurried certain of his officers, expostulating and explaining.

"Who goes there? Eh, it is you, young Desnouettes?" the Emperor cried, as the boy sprang from the saddle. "Well, what news? what news?"

"Nothing but what you have already heard, Sire," Philip

replied, sadly. "We fought like tigers, but the Cossacks were too much for us. Ah, had you but been there, Sire!"

"Yes, yes; I know—I know. But one cannot be everywhere," Napoleon said, flicking the ground with his riding-whip, as was his wont when he was perplexed or excited. "But now it is no time for complaints; now it is time to act. We must repair the evil. Run, my Philip; run to the post-house. Bid them hurry up my carriage. Every one is an imbecile to-day. Why are they so slow? Come! my carriage, my carriage, my carriage!"

It was almost King Richard's despairing cry repeated: "A horse! a horse! my kingdom for a horse!"

"But it is too late, Sire," Philip explained. "The enemy is already in Paris."

"What!—you too?" the Emperor cried. "You are all singing the same song. Suppose he is—I am going there, too. I will lead on my army, and drive the enemy from Paris—my Paris! my Paris!" he repeated. "Forward, gentlemen! Let us clear out the barbarians!"

"Too late, Sire," said General Belliard, the leader of the cavalry advance. "Our troops are marching away from the city. We cannot go back. We have signed a capitulation."

"A capitulation!" the Emperor blazed out. "Who has been so cowardly?"

"No cowards, Sire," Belliard replied. "Brave men who could not do otherwise."

Still Napoleon walked on toward Paris. Still he called again and again for his carriage. Still his generals followed at his heels. Then other soldiers advanced toward him. The same questions were asked: the same replies given.

And the Emperor, realizing at last that his wish indeed was hopeless, flung himself upon the stone seat that flanked the fountain of Juvisy and buried his face in his hands. All were silent. No one broke in upon the crowding thoughts that marked the tearless anguish of a conquered conqueror.

At last he rose. Calm succeeded to despair. Dignity, composure, energy, came again to the face that so seldom betrayed emotion.

Then reaction came. Napoleon had ridden nearly two hundred miles without rest, and all to no purpose. Going into the little posting-house near to the fountain, he dropped into a chair and, for an instant, rested his head upon the table. But, no! He must not sleep; he must work. He called for lights. He spread out his war-maps upon the table, and sticking his pins here and there, as was his custom, at once began to study the situation. Philip never forgot that scene—the gray of the morning, the group of silent soldiers, and, through the open door of the cottage, in the circle of flickering light, the tired and defeated leader of men poring over his maps, planning a new campaign.

But that campaign never came. Fate was too strong for him; and, yielding to the inevitable, Napoleon finally gave up his determination to make an instant march on Paris with the troops who were following him from the eastern frontier, and rode wearily to his palace at Fontainebleau, a few miles to the south. There he would rest; there he would plan things more carefully; and, calling around him his scattered battalions, he would mass them for an irresistible march on his foes, whom he declared he now had "trapped in Paris."

Bad news travels quickly. And bad news speedily found its way to Fontainebleau. The allies entered Paris. The city—"faithful Paris," as the Emperor had called it—instead of rising against the invaders, welcomed them. France was weary of war. The dignitaries of the Empire, following the lead of Talleyrand, "that arch-conspirator," one by one deserted the Emperor who had made them rich and loaded them with honors. They gave in their allegiance to the new government. The white cockade and the white flag of the Bourbons appeared on the streets. "Long live the King!" began to be heard where "Long live the Emperor!" had so often been shouted. The abdication of the Emperor was demanded, and fickle Paris ran easily down the scale from homage to nickname, from the Emperor to Napoleon—Bonaparte—"the Corsican"—"Nicholas!"—until at last it made ready to welcome back the Bourbons, whom a generation before it had hacked to death on the guillotine and driven away in the days of terror.

Treason hastened the work. Napoleon's army, upon which he had depended for his revenge, dwindled away; and Marmont—brave Marmont, who had so valiantly defended Paris—went over with his entire army corps, and for ever after was esteemed a traitor by the France he hoped to serve and save.

The marshals, whom the Emperor had raised to rank and riches, joined in the cry for his abdication. They conspired against their old leader; it is claimed they even doomed him to death if he refused to obey their will.

Thus, deserted by his companions-in-arms, worn out with a useless struggle—loath, now, to plunge France into civil war by appeals to the people who were loyal and the old soldiers who were faithful to him — Napoleon, with that serenity that marks a great soul, yielded to the inevitable, and, on the eleventh of April, 1814, signed his abdication as Emperor of the French, and quietly stepped down from the high position he so long had occupied. It was the noblest act of his life, even though men might say it was compulsory.

This is the act of renunciation he signed — this victor, vanquished by Fate, and by his own ambition:

The Allied Powers having proclaimed that the Emperor is the sole obstacle to the reëstablishment of peace in Europe, the Emperor, faithful to his oath, declares that he renounces for himself and for his family the thrones of France and Italy, and that there is no sacrifice, even to that of his life, which he is not ready to make for the interests of France.

The tricolor had indeed fallen. The man who, for so many years, had given glory and greatness to France, who had distracted England with war, startled the whole Continent with his success, and filled the world with his name, stepped down from his throne, and Europe once more breathed freely. Great in everything he did, Napoleon was as great in his fall as in his glory. The Empire was dead.

Through all these days of watching and waiting, of planning and plotting, of hopes and fears, Philip stood by the Emperor, serving him as best he could, riding to Paris, bearing messages — now to the friends and now to the foes of the man he clung to alike in victory and defeat.

He stood by the Emperor's bedside, that sad night on which, for the only time in his life, Napoleon played the coward and tried to commit suicide. He was near him that famous morning when in the Court of the White Horse, in the beautiful palace of Fontainebleau, Napoleon bade farewell to his Old Guard, and left for the island principality that had been given him as his home—it was almost a prison—the little island of Elba, in the Mediterranean.

That was the moment when Philip's pent-up feelings had overflowed, and the tears he would not have checked if he could came tumbling down his cheeks. Already the Emperor had said farewell to this boy who had so faithfully served him.

Standing in the splendid gallery of Francis I., which opens upon the famous Horseshoe Staircase, down which Napoleon walked to say good-by to his Guard, the boy had begged and implored the Emperor to let him be one of the chosen four hundred soldiers who were to accompany the dethroned monarch to his tiny island realm.

But, "No, my Philip," the Emperor said, "it cannot be. Go home to your dear ones, the sister you have found, the good Citizen Daunou, who is like a father to you. There lies your duty—to them and to France. Serve France, my son, as loyally as you have served me; and when she needs your strong young arm and that sometimes flighty but always truth-telling tongue of yours, I know she will not call in vain."

Then Napoleon passed on amid his officers, down the Horseshoe Staircase and into the White Horse Court.

The drums beat a salute. Then they were silent, and Napoleon, in a voice first strong, then broken and full of feeling, said farewell to his stalwart soldiers of the Guard, his never-failing reliance on every field of battle.

It was one of the most pathetic moments in history. Every man was thrilled; and when, breaking off his speech, Napoleon flung his arms about the standard-bearer, grasped the imperial standard and touched his lips to the eagle that crowned it, Emperor, generals, soldiers, all were in tears.

Philip clung to the step of the carriage. Tears blinded the bright young eyes that looked up to his master in the final farewell. The Emperor placed a hand upon his head. "Good-by, my boy. God bless you!" he said. Then the horses started; the carriage rolled out of the courtyard, and to Philip it seemed as if all the glory, all the promise, and all the pride of living passed from his brave young life.

But boys rally quickly, even from deeper sorrows. Philip returned to the Street of the Fight, proud and happy over the Emperor's words of praise, and delighted to find that this pathetic "Passing of Napoleon" had conquered even the stout old republican, who had served his Emperor faithfully, even when he most questioned the imperial measures. For now the old Keeper of the Archives looked upon the fallen monarch almost as devotedly as did the hero-worshiping boy and girl who brightened his quiet home.

The tricolor had fallen. The white standard waved above the Tuileries. The Bourbons returned to power. Old Louis XVIII. was king of France, and those who had served the bees took service under the lilies.

But this Philip stoutly refused to do. One day, Citizen Daunou said: "My son, you can be a page of the palace still, if you wish. The King recalls your father's services in the days before the Republic. He knows how he died, and he will gladly give the son of Desnouettes the *émigré*

THE FALL OF THE TRICOLOR 257

a place of honor in his train." Then Philip replied, unhesitatingly, "I cannot; I cannot, my father. The Emperor found me poor and friendless. He stood me on my

"THE EMPEROR PLACED A HAND UPON HIS HEAD."

feet; he tried to make a man of me. While he lives, there is for me no other king. I would not be page to the Bourbons for all the gold in their palaces. If ever the foreigner threatens France I will remember the Emperor's charge, and serve France as well as I may; but never the Bourbons! Let me, rather, if I may, stay here with you and Mademoiselle, my sister."

"There spake my boy," Citizen Daunou said; and Mademoiselle kissed her brother tenderly and cried, "There is no truer friend than our Philip, is there, my father?"

The days passed by. France accepted the Bourbons. Paris paid court to them. There were fêtes and receptions, balls and illuminations, processions, shows, and displays, even as there had been in the Empire days—though there were people who said these could not compare with those for magnificence. But in all such doings Philip had neither interest nor part. He took up the studies he had dropped when the stress of France called him to ride and write for the Emperor. He perfected himself in military science, and the drawing and mathematics which delighted him. Citizen Daunou praised him highly for this.

"Be strong in your mathematical study, Philip, my boy," he said. "That best tries a boy's patience and builds up a boy's brain. I wish I had your head for figures."

Whereat Philip laughed; for he thought Citizen Daunou knew everything. He laughed, also, it must be confessed, when he heard the notes of discontent that were growing each day louder over what folks called "the mistakes of the Bourbons," and he discussed many times with Citizen Daunou, and sometimes with clever young Mademoiselle, the embarrassment of the new government, the disputes of royalists and republicans, the discontent of the army, and the attempts of the famous "Congress of Vienna" to straighten out the mixed-up affairs of Europe.

Even the good old Keeper of the Archives was sometimes "out of sorts" and disgusted at the things that were going on. He said one day to Philip, "After all, Napoleon was but right when he declared, 'The Bourbons will reconcile France with the rest of Europe, but set her at war with herself.' You will see; you will see!"

Philip especially enjoyed hunting up Corporal Peyrolles and having a good talk with him. The old veteran was a bitter partizan. To him the marshals were renegades; the dignitaries who had accepted the Bourbons were traitors; the Bourbons were knaves and cowards.

"Look now at that old pig of a Capet, Philip!" he cried —for to the old soldier of the Revolution the brother of Louis XVI. was, like that unfortunate, no king, but only a man whose name was Capet—"Look on him, riding the very streets our Emperor has trod. An invalid, say you? Yes, but not from wounds like those of us who have dropped our blood for France! An invalid, he, from age, with never a touch of glory. What is he, then? A puppet show worked by Cossacks."

Then, in high glee, Peyrolles pulled from his pocket one of the comic pictures of the day. "Look you, my boy. Here is that Capet. This is he!" And Philip laughed, too, at the rudely-colored picture of old King Louis XVIII. riding behind a hairy Cossack on a sorry-looking horse, and hugging the barbarian tightly for fear of falling off. But both the boy and the veteran stamped with rage at sight of the highway over which Cossack and King were riding—the bodies of French soldiers who had died for the Emperor.

Peyrolles, by this time, was an inmate of the Soldiers'

Home—that splendid building with the magnificent dome, then called the Temple of Mars, but famous now as the great Hotel of the Invalids. The old corporal had no objection to being cared for there. "For," said he, "the Emperor sent me there, and it is the money of France and not of the Bourbons that pays for my keeping."

Here Philip would often visit the veteran; and here, one February day in the year 1815, he and Mademoiselle had made their weekly call upon the old soldier. Their talk had been of Uncle Fauriel and of Pierre—of Pierre who had lost his place in their good graces because he had continued as police inspector after the Bourbons had returned to power.

"One can see," said Philip, "how one may hold on to his place in a civil bureau, as does Citizen Daunou, or live at the Soldiers' Home, as do you, Peyrolles, after the Bourbons have come in; but how one can serve on their police,—those who must do their dirty work, you know,—as Pierre is serving, is more than I can understand."

All of which is drawing a fine distinction; but opinions as to office-holding often admit of fine distinctions—even in other countries than France—and Philip therefore felt justified in saying, "No, I cannot understand it. I am disappointed in Pierre!"

With Mademoiselle, that February day, he had left the Soldiers' Home and had taken a roundabout way for their return, extending their walk into Philip's old quarter, from which the Emperor had rescued him—the Fourth Ward of Paris and the Street of the Washerwomen.

At the identical fountain, at the foot of that narrow and

dirty street, where Philip and Pierre had fought their famous fight,—it seemed to Philip as if that were ages ago, Philip and Mademoiselle stopped for a moment to look at a detachment of troops marching from the barriers to the military bureau in the Place Vendôme. Philip winced as he looked at them, as he always winced—for they were no longer the soldiers of the Emperor; they were the soldiers of the King. The white flag instead of the tricolor was borne in their ranks; the white cockade instead of the tricolor decorated their shakos; the white of the Kingdom rather than the blue of the Empire predominated in their uniforms.

The people in the poorer quarters of Paris, never enthusiastic for the King,—recalling the days when they and their fathers had put down this very race of Bourbons,—had no ringing shout of "Long live the King!" as, they had once shouted "Long live the Emperor!"

So the watching throng about the fountain was silent or sarcastic. But it was an uneasy crowd. It jostled and swayed and pushed, and Philip was forced to grasp Mademoiselle closely for her security. Gradually they were forced back against the stone coping of the fountain, and, as Philip struggled to maintain his own footing and save Mademoiselle from a crushing, he was startled almost to stupidity to hear a low but distinct whisper in his ear: "Be watchful and wary! The eagle will swoop on the geese. Be swift and silent. The bees will soon be swarming!"

What did it mean? Who had spoken such a singular message. Philip turned slowly, not wishing to attract attention. But to no purpose. The only familiar face he saw was that of his sister. What could it mean?

CHAPTER XXI

THE SWARMING OF THE BEES

FOR a moment Philip was too bewildered to speak. Then he turned a white face toward his sister.

"Who was that?" he asked her.

Mademoiselle was intently watching the vanishing ranks of the white cockades. Philip repeated his question. Mademoiselle looked puzzled.

"Who was who, my Philip?" she queried.

"Why, did you see no one? Did you hear nothing?" Philip asked in a voice trembling with surprise and excitement.

"Why, my Philip, what can you mean?" the girl replied. "What has startled you? I saw none save the soldiers yonder. I heard nothing but the people all about us."

"What was it, then? It is all very strange, this!" her brother murmured, only half aloud. Then he said suddenly: "What was the picture we laughed over so — you and I — a few days ago, Mademoiselle? The one Corporal Peyrolles brought us?"

Mademoiselle rounded her pretty lips in thought. "A picture?" she said. "What, then — do you mean that one where those funny fat geese were waddling up the steps of the Tuileries, and an eagle was flying away from the dome?"

"Yes, yes; that was it," Philip answered. "The geese and the eagle? How odd! But can it be so, then? And why the bees?"

Philip pushed his chapeau back upon his head, and gave a long, low whistle through his half-closed teeth. Mademoiselle looked anxious; she began to fear something was the trouble with her vivacious brother.

"What do you mean, you Philip?" she asked him. "What is odd? Can what be so? Why do you whistle? And why that picture?"

"Something I have just heard," was Philip's unsatisfactory reply. "Let me think; let — me — think. I will tell you later."

Mademoiselle possessed all the curiosity which, we are assured, is the privilege of her sex. Philip had a secret; she must know what it was. So she grew more and more inquisitive as they hurried home; but her brother answered her not a word in explanation until they were safely within the house on the Street of the Fight. Then he sought out Citizen Daunou, and told him the story of the mysterious message.

The worthy Keeper of the Archives rubbed his white head thoughtfully.

"You were dreaming, boy," he said; "or else the whisper was but a Fourth Ward joke. They raise but rattlepates, you know, there in the Street of the Washerwomen. As, for example"; and he clapped Philip on the shoulder.

But the boy was in no mood for pleasantry. "Dreaming

or awake, joke or no, my father, I heard the words," he declared. Then he added swiftly, "Which way, now, lies this Elba?"

It was now Citizen Daunou's turn to look startled.

"Elba?" he said. "Why, to the southeast some two hundred leagues or so. But why do you ask?"

Mademoiselle, who had stolen in to hear, was even quicker-witted. She clasped her brother close.

"To Elba, Philip?" she cried. "You would surely not go there. And why?"

"Where the bees swarm and the eagle soars," said the boy, more theatrically than he really intended, "there is the place for him who with the bees would swarm and who would soar with the eagle!"

"My faith, Philip!" exclaimed practical Mademoiselle. "But what is all this we hear about bees and eagles? Does it mean — What? does it, now?— the Emperor?"

"It does! it does, my sister!" Philip cried, flushed with ardor and excitement. "Let not your tongue speak the wonderful message outside this house. The Emperor is coming back!"

"Philip!" the girl exclaimed, catching her brother's excitement. "My father, is this so?"

Philip nodded energetically. And Citizen Daunou said, "It may be but a joke of the Washerwomen's quarter to stir up our Philip here, as I have told him; but yet — nothing is impossible to Napoleon. Nothing can surprise me in the ways of that wonderful man. Pray heaven he does not come, even though France calls him and all men marvel at him! It will be a terrible mistake. No good can come of it. Better let the Bourbons unhorse themselves by their own blundering than that France should be ruined by a profitless frenzy and a dream of glory that can lead only to ruin."

"But the Emperor is coming, you say?" Mademoiselle repeated, heedless of the old man's moralizing. "Why, men tell us he is peaceful and satisfied there at Elba, and has no desire to return."

Citizen Daunou shook his head in disbelief. "They are but fools who say it, then," he replied. "Napoleon is no Diocletian — an emperor out of business, content to raise his own cabbages at Salona; he is no Charles V., resigned to patter prayers at St. Just. The world is not done with when one is but forty-five; and abdication does not kill ambition. The Emperor has not yet fed full of war and glory. Elba is all too small a world for him to govern, and he will tire of it, if he has not already done so. The Eagle will beat his wings until he breaks his cage bars, and will try a flight to Notre Dame. I know his ambition; it is boundless. But such a flight will never succeed. Once again the Eagle may flap his wings above the dome of the Tuileries; but the fowling-piece that kills crows may bring down an eagle, and the hunters will speedily be abroad. Let Napoleon stay on his island, or die in escaping from it; his mission for France is ended. Fontainebleau was his climax. To return would be but anti-climax; and that is always a mistake, is it not, you boy of the Paris schools?"

No doubt the wise old scholar was right. But Mademoiselle could not admit it; and Philip surely would not. When did youth ever neglect to bow before glory, or refuse to yield to the spell of adventure? Great thoughts were stirring in the boy's busy brain; high hopes were surging in his brave young heart.

"Brush up my very best page suit, Mademoiselle my sister," he said; "and keep it ready for use. Citizen Daunou, I crave your permission to go on a quest. Within a week I will be with you again."

"'A boy's will is the wind's will,'" the quiet old Keeper remarked. "'T is a fool's errand, Philip, but I cannot say no to you. Only — guard yourself, my son; be not rash. Remember what I told you — the hunters will speedily be abroad, if your message at the fountain was a true tale. Guard yourself for Mademoiselle's sake, for my sake, for France!"

And within two hours' time Philip had left his dear ones in the Street of the Fight, and was off to the southward.

The whispered message by the fountain in the Street of the Washerwomen was not a dream. It was a fact. The Emperor had escaped from Elba. He was on his way to France.

He risked his head to recover his throne; and France — fickle France — flamed out to welcome him back, though it knew his return might mean disturbance, distress, even war and death once more.

Philip met the truth at Lyons. The air was full of rumors that speedily became facts. With less than a thousand of his grenadiers — his "brave growlers" as he sometimes called them — the Emperor had landed in France. The army had gone over to him, wild with joy. The Empire would be proclaimed once more. France would be free of the Bourbons.

Philip found Lyons in a ferment. Napoleon was almost at its gates. The Bourbon prince who commanded the troops gathered at that important city ordered his soldiers to the wall to repel or capture "the bandit from Elba." But what was a Bourbon prince before "our Emperor?"

The tidings of the imperial adventurer came thick and fast. Napoleon had landed near Cannes; he had marched over the mountains to Dijon; he had first fronted the white standard with his tricolor at Laffrey; with bared breast he had faced the soldiers of the King in the Vale of Beaumont, bidding them welcome him or kill him; and behold! the soldiers of the King had fallen on their knees before him, cried "Long live the Emperor!" and hailed him as their "father." He had kissed the restored eagles at Vizelle; he had entered Grenoble, through the gates burst open by the peasants without and the revolted soldiers within; escorted by mountaineers and farmers singing the Marseilles hymn, he had advanced from Grenoble to Lyons with his little "army of deliverance," already grown from one thousand to six thousand soldiers, wearing the tricolored cockade. Off hurries the Bourbon prince in terror of his life; down go the barricades, wrecked by the very soldiers who had piled them up; "Long live the Emperor!" shout garrison and citizens; and to the accompaniment of twenty thousand welcoming voices Napoleon enters Lyons.

And there, on the steps of the Archbishop's palace, to which the Emperor was conducted, Philip greeted him with tears and laughter and a voice thrilling with passionate welcome.

"What?—is it you, young Desnouettes?" the Emperor

cried, catching the page around the neck. "My brave boy, is it you?"

"Yes, from Paris, Sire," answered the boy; "to greet you and die for you."

"No; live for me; live for me, you Philip," the Emperor said. "And what do they say at Paris?"

"Sire, I did not wait to hear," answered truthful Philip. "I ran to join you as soon as they whispered that you had left for France."

"As heedless as ever; eh, you boy?" and then came the ear-pinching that seemed so like old times come again. "Well; to me, to me, my Philip! I shall have duties for you."

Three days the Emperor rested at Lyons, reviewing his troops, organizing his government, writing despatches, and sending broadcast over France those two masterly proclamations that are so marked a specimen of Napoleonic eloquence and so rich a combination of sublimity, sentiment, metaphor, and,— it must be admitted,— what we should call "the highfalutin."

Philip galloped from Lyons a day in advance of the Emperor, bearing messages to the friends of Napoleon in Paris, and spreading the wonderful tidings as he rode. France seemed wild with joy. Down went the white cockade; up went the tricolor; the Emperor's flower—the violet—blossomed in countless buttonholes. The lilies drooped: the bees were swarming everywhere.

Philip burst into the quiet house on the Street of the Fight and filled it with his wonderful news.

"He has come; he has come back!" he shouted. "I have seen the Emperor!"

Mademoiselle laughed and cried in her excitement; Nurse Marcel tore off her bonne's cap and waved it frantically: "Down go the aristocrats!" she shrilled out. Citizen Daunou, forgetting his philosophy, pounded on the table and shouted "Long live the Emperor!" Marshal, the big Dane, put off his dignity, and barked and capered like any thoughtless young puppy; and Philip, seizing the page's livery that Mademoiselle thrust into his restless hands, kissed them all excitedly, not omitting even the vociferous Marshal, and rushed off to the Tuileries.

"Eh, you boy! Hurrah, young Desnouettes! Where so fast, now? I told you the truth, did I not?" Philip paused in his running long enough to recognize his questioner.

"What is it, you, Pierre?" he cried. "Long live the — what do you mean, though? You told the truth? What, then — was it you?"

"At the fountain, yonder? To be sure," Pierre said composedly. "I have known what was afoot for many a day. Oh, we know something at headquarters, now and then.

"And you did not seek to stop him? Oh, Pierre! and I thought you a royalist and a renegade. Kick me, Pierre. It is your right. How could I have doubted you?" Philip was almost hysterical in his mixture of surprise and joy, as, repentant and rejoicing, he fell upon Pierre.

"We who know how to open our ears and hold our tongues, Monsieur the page, Monsieur the lieutenant, can sometimes work our ways better than those who grumble and shout," the young inspector said. "Those who chatter, too often dance with the sky-mother;[1] and, faith, I have no

[1] The Paris boy's name for the terrible guillotine.

liking for her. Yes, I dropped that word of warning into your ear at our old fountain, and then vanished. It was all I dared do, then. But it worked, I see, it worked. And you are for—?"

"The Tuileries, Pierre. See me again, my friend. I would get there before the Emperor," and in a flash Philip was speeding again toward the Tuileries.

As he reached the palace, soldiers and veterans were filling the Place of the Carrousel. Among the latter Philip was not surprised to see old Corporal Peyrolles, proud and radiant.

The veteran from the Soldiers' Home swung his cocked hat, graced with the tricolored cockade, and brought his cane to the salute, as Philip greeted him.

"Death of my life, my infant!" the old man cried, his gruff voice breaking in a high key; "but is not this glorious? Look at us here—Arcola, the Pyramids, Marengo, Austerlitz, Wagram, Lutzen, Moscow, and the Clichy Gate! we are all here; and he is coming. Wait till he sees me. I'll put him on the throne if I have to prop it up with my wooden leg, here. Open the palace! Pull down the white rag! Out with old Grandfather In-the-soup! In with Corporal Violet!"[1]

And all the old veterans tuned their cracked voices into the mighty yell: "Down with the white flag! Long live the Little Corporal!"

Sure enough, to Philip's amazement and the old soldiers' disgust, the white flag of the Bourbons still floated from the

[1] "Father Panade" and "Corporal Violet" were soldiers' names for Louis XVIII. and Napoleon.

Clock Tower of the Tuileries. King Louis had fled, but there was still a show of resistance from the National Guardsmen he had left in the palace.

It is two in the afternoon. The increasing throng grows more insistent. The growls of the veterans, the shouts of the soldiers, become ominous and threatening. Then a great cry goes up. The gates are thrown open. Another shout. Down goes the white flag; up goes the tricolor; and, as the Imperial banner once again streams from the great Clock Tower, all Paris knows that the Bourbons have given up the struggle, and that the Empire has won.

Evening came — that eventful evening of Monday, the twentieth of March, in the year 1815. The Tuileries was filled with guests dressed as if for a fête night. Those who were in hiding, and those who had deserted King Louis, met to await the coming of the Emperor. The great mansion blazed with lights, and a page of the palace, resplendent in his imperial livery, with almost beside himself for joy.

It was Philip Desnouettes. He had seen the Emperor. He had been charged by him with messages to Paris. Philip was the lion of the waiting hours. He was petted and praised by every one. He began to feel very important once more.

He could scarcely contain himself. He wished to keep busy, to be doing something to prove his devotion.

The palace looked just the same. Philip could scarcely believe that a year had passed since he had been there. "Here are the same hangings," he said to himself; "the same stiff, straight furniture, the same bureaus and cabinets, tête-à-têtes, couches and chairs, decorated with their brass or ormolu wreaths and festoons, sphinxes, and victories, and sprinkled with the—no! Halls! What is this? The lilies? Then where are the bees? Have the royalists dared remove from the palace decorations the bees of Napoleon, and put in their place the lilies of the Bourbons? Why, this will never do!"

Frantic with indignant loyalty, Philip shouted: "Off with the lilies — on with the bees!" and falling upon the unoffending decorations, Philip, helped by many ready hands, tore down the lilies from the tapestry, and stripped them from the coverings. From some hiding-place were brought the hangings that bore the bees, and reawakened loyalty was satisfied.

At nine o'clock a mighty shout was heard without.

"The Emperor! the Emperor!"

The palace echoed the cry, as, across the Bridge of the Palace and along the Seine embankment, in through the Tuileries gate, thronged about by a clamorous crowd, and surrounded by his soldiers and his generals, Napoleon entered the courtyard of the great palace.

Then it seemed as if Paris had indeed gone mad. The veterans flung themselves at the Emperor's carriage. They seized their hero in their arms. They dragged him out; and, bearing him on their shoulders, they rushed with him through the doorway even to the foot of the great staircase.

The palace rocked with the shouts of welcome. The crowd bearing in the Emperor, and the throng pouring down the staircase to greet him, blocked the way. Progress was impossible. People were everywhere, and Philip, standing at the

"'OFF WITH THE LILIES—ON WITH THE BEES!'"

top of the noble Stairway of Honor, laughed as he cheered, to see Corporal Peyrolles sitting astride the great silver statue of Peace, his chapeau waving at the end of his cane, his face red with shouting and streaked with tears of joy.

At last a passage-way was broken through the crowd. Philip and Monsieur de Lavalette backed their way aloft to keep the passage open; and so, up the clamoring stairway, along the Gallery of Diana, through the Blue Room, and into the Emperor's study, amid tears and cheers and shouts, and tossing of hats, and waving of handkerchiefs, the Emperor came to his own again. In twenty days after leaving Elba Napoleon had regained his empire. With but a thousand grenadiers he had conquered thirty millions of people. The swarming of the Bees closed in a carnival of joy.

In the Emperor's study, breathless and weeping with the excitement of the home-coming, Napoleon looked about him. The closed doors of the study shut out the happy crowd. At his feet he saw a kneeling figure, dressed in the crimson, green, and gold of a page of the palace.

"What, it is you again, my Philip!" exclaimed the Emperor. "And in your page's livery. Rise, my boy. You are a page no longer. Such devotion merits a higher service. See; my fortune shall be yours! Did I not tell you once that he who rides and he who writes merit often as much esteem as he who bears the musket or wields the sword? I make you a member of the Legion of Honor. Here, Bertrand, Lavalette, some one — give me a cross! What! none will spare me one?" No one would. Crosses of the Legion were to be displayed just then; they were treasured too highly to be given to a boy. "Here then!" and impulsively

the Emperor tore the cherished decoration from his own
breast, pinned it on the lad's green coat, and pinching his

THE EMPEROR DECORATES PHILIP WITH HIS OWN CROSS OF THE
LEGION OF HONOR.

ear affectionately, cried to General Bertrand, who stood beside him, "Grand Marshal, here is a new officer of my household! *Captain* Desnouettes — page and lieutenant no longer,

— you are a brevet-officer, specially attached to my person. Serve me as comrade as faithfully as you have as page, and France shall be proud of you."

And, while the boy trembled with delight and pride, the Emperor caught him to his breast and kissed him on the cheek.

So Philip, by a faithfulness that never faltered, and a loyalty that never wavered, gained the prize all Frenchmen coveted.

Thus he won the Cross.

CHAPTER XXII

"INTO THE FURNACE-FLAME"

AT once Philip was head over ears in business. If the Emperor was gracious and appreciative, he was also a hard taskmaster when work was to be done. And there was work unending to be done when, once again, in the palaces of Paris, the imperial government was in active operation. Day and night Napoleon, desiring peace, but preparing for war, was closeted in consultation with his ministers.

His return from Elba flamed like a comet in the skies of Europe. Kings were startled, princes trembled, allies who had deserted and foes who had plotted against him read vengeance in his return; and with a united growl of rage the nations of Europe combined for his overthrow. All the sovereigns signed that declaration of hate and terror, drawn up by a Frenchman whom Napoleon had loaded with favors, which proclaimed to the world that "Napoleon Bonaparte, by reappearing in France, is placed outside of all relations, both civil and social, and, as an enemy and disturber of the peace of the world, he is handed over to public vengeance."

Thus did the kings and ministers who once had bowed in homage to the Emperor now proclaim him outlaw and outcast. Napoleon sought peace with all nations. He wished only to unite France.

"The first desire of my heart," he wrote to the kings of Europe, "is to repay the affection of my people by maintaining an honorable tranquillity."

And when told that one of the Bourbon princes would perhaps be captured in France, he said, "If so, treat him with every respect. I wish that Europe should see the difference between me and the crowned brigands who have set a price upon my head."

But though he worked and wished for peace, he knew he must prepare for war. All Europe was arming against him. France must be ready to resist.

So the Emperor and those about him worked day and night. They worked until even Philip's vigorous nature gave out, and one night, set to a certain task, weariness got the better of ability, his head dropped upon the table before him, and the secretary slept at his post.

How long he slept he did not know, but he awoke with a start to see the Emperor in a chair beside him, doing his work for him.

Mortified beyond measure Philip sprang to his feet. The Emperor wrote on. Then he said to the secretary:

"Well, sir, you see I have been doing your work, since you would not do it yourself. No doubt you had a hearty supper at Tortoni's or the Thousand Columns, and after that a good time with the other boys. It was all very pleasant, no doubt; but that is no excuse. Business is business and must not be neglected."

"A good time! I, Sire?" exclaimed honest Philip. "Does this look like it? I have worked for your majesty night and day; I have scarcely had a full night's sleep in a week, and this is the consequence. I am sorry for it, Sire. I ask your pardon."

It was now the Emperor who was moved. "My poor boy!" he said. "I did not know of this. My Philip, I am no slave-driver. I have no wish to kill you. A healthy boy needs his sleep. Go to bed; go to bed at once, sir. Good night to you!"

But Philip pleaded to remain and retrieve himself, protesting his ability to work now that he had stolen a nap; and the Emperor, laughing, said, "Well, Captain Philip, we will compromise; we two. Do this bit, and then get you to bed. Copy this draft of a decree. You can read my villainous handwriting and we need not wait for Baron Fain. I wish to issue it at once. I told you but now, did I not, that I was no slave-driver? This, too, will prove it."

And in the still hours of that March night, in the Emperor's study at the Tuileries, Philip copied, and Napoleon signed, a paper which undid the Bourbons' feudal brutality, anticipated the ponderous pens of the slow-going diplomats of the Vienna Congress which had declared him an outlaw, and gave to the "hundred days" of Napoleon's fleeting second reign a glory which the world has not yet sufficiently acknowledged—the decree abolishing forever in all the colonies of France the hateful and degrading slave-trade.

Philip, it must be confessed, thought but little of this act of justice, which the nations tardily followed. But when, dismissed for his sleep, upon which the Emperor insisted, he went, later, to breakfast with his sister, Citizen Dannou hailed the news of the Emperor's decree with delight.

"I take back my words," the liberty-loving Keeper of the

Archives said. "I told you no good could come of the Emperor's flight from Elba. I was wrong. Good has come of it. For, if he shall accomplish nothing else, he has reaffirmed the principles of the Republic and set the world a lesson in liberty. Toussaint l'Ouverture is avenged by the very man who, years ago, crushed that black patriot beneath his imperial will."

The days went on. In Europe a million men were arming for the fray that all the world saw was inevitable. In France, the Emperor was preparing for resistance. The old regiments were filled up. The veterans drew from their hiding-places at the bottom of knapsacks or inside their drums the discarded tricolor they would not throw away, and hastened to rally around the eagles; the conscripts gathered at the stations with knapsacks, cartridge-box, and musket. Steadily and surely the day of Waterloo drew near.

"The flag we have dyed with our blood will lead us again to glory!" cried Corporal Peyrolles, turning to his own use the words of his Emperor's proclamation. But Mademoiselle, always practical, declared she could not see how Corporal Peyrolles could do any more than stump along to glory, and that for her part she thought it would be best for him to stay at home and protect Paris while the Emperor faced the foreigners. It would be too distracting for the Emperor, she said, if Peyrolles were along; for, of course, the Corporal would wish to run things, and that, she declared, would be quite too confusing and would read so oddly in the bulletins. Whereupon Corporal Peyrolles called her a saucy minx, but admitted that he thought himself quite as competent to advise the Emperor as those dukes and marshals he still kept about him.

"Let but Philip get speech for me with the Emperor," the Corporal protested, "and I will show him how to get rid of these pigs of Prussians, these curs of Englishmen, these beasts of Russians. Take 'em on the flank, take 'em on the flank, I say. Why, at the Pyramids— no, it was before Jaffa— I said to the Emperor— he was not Emperor then, you know— I said to him, 'My General,' said I—"

But Mademoiselle saucily pulled the Corporal's long moustache and ran away. "That is what the Emperor did, my Corporal, did he not now —at the Pyramids—no, it was before Jaffa," she cried merrily; and then left poor old Peyrolles fuming over the "heedlessness of these women," who always will "spoil a good story," so he grumbled.

The invaders of France gathered beyond its borders; the defenders of France marched to the frontiers. The Emperor, professing his desire only to promote the good of France, granted a new constitution which would give greater liberty to the people, and held, on the Field of Mars, fronting the flashing Seine, a splendid fête and open-air display, still famous as the gorgeous "Field of May." There on his throne, surrounded by his brothers and his great officers of state, Napoleon reviewed his fifty thousand troops and aroused the cheers of the people, always ready to enjoy a show in which glitter and gorgeousness and imperial splendor, music and marching, and all the theatrical accessories were spread before their eyes with all the old-time magnificence.

Seated upon his throne, the Emperor reviewed his troops,

received the electors and dignitaries of the Empire, and swore allegiance to the new constitution.

"Frenchmen!" he said, "my will is that of the people. My rights are theirs. My honor, my glory, my happiness cannot be other than the honor, the glory, the happiness of France.

"Soldiers! I confide to you the imperial eagle of the national colors. Swear to defend it with your blood against the enemies of the fatherland. Swear to die rather than to suffer strangers to make laws for the fatherland."

And all the soldiers cried, "We swear it!" and the people shouted "Long live the Emperor!"

But the enemies of France were marching; the "strangers" were coming to bring blood and ruin to the fatherland. The shadow of the conflict seemed already to rest upon the imperial adventurer throned in his splendid palace of the Tuileries.

"Is not the Emperor glorious?" cried enthusiastic Philip, after the gorgeous ceremonial of the Field of May was over, as he walked into the dear house in the Street of the Fight. "Was not that fête magnificent?"

"Call it a funeral rather than a fête, my son," Citizen Daunou said, sadly. His momentary enthusiasm after the Emperor's dramatic return was gone. His clear vision saw the trouble that was in store for France. "And the Emperor? Glorious, perhaps, as you say, with his imperial robes and his words of fire. But to me he is no longer the Emperor of 1810. His counselors are nerveless; they are timid; to me, they seem to have the vertigo. He, alas! is languid; only on great occasions does the old spirit flame out. He seems full of melancholy. His haughtiness has softened almost to entreaty; his pride to gentleness. Good signs if all were well, my Philip; but all is not well, my Philip. The Emperor sees the shadow of failure. France is noisy in her crowds; she is vociferous in her soldiers; but this is not the zeal Napoleon hoped for — is not the zeal of a united nation. His enemies are pitiless; his friends are uncertain. He has no ally, no vassal, no imperial power. He wishes peace, he must have war. How will that end?"

Philip, as usual, scoffed in his heart at this gloomy picture, and expressed to Mademoiselle the wish that Citizen Daunou were more patriotic. "Why does he talk of failure?" the boy demanded. "The Emperor cannot fail. The army and the nation are at his back. Defeated? Never! That is no way for a Frenchman to talk. I really must bring Peyrolles here again to reason with our excellent father."

Boys and girls can seldom go beneath the surface of things, as do their elders. And it is well, perhaps; for youth is the time of hope. Philip certainly saw none of the signs of sadness that Citizen Daunou detected. "Just let him work beside the Emperor for a day as I do," the boy declared, "and my faith! it is he that will be the sad one—from too much work." To Philip the Emperor was still the Emperor—great, powerful, victorious, invincible. Philip knew that he would conquer; that once again he would give the law to Europe. This, each day, was the burden of the brave boy's song.

The work increased in the palace, as the time for the conflict approached. Napoleon had done marvels. Within two months he had raised, equipped, and officered an army of three hundred thousand men. Arsenals, factories, and military shops were busy; trade was good; business was flourishing. What more could France wish?

Philip, growing older and more observant, saw and treasured up many of the ways of this remarkable man, upon whom the eyes of the world were fixed. Many times in after years would he recall the picture of the Emperor in those last busy mornings in his study—the stout, short-legged, long-bodied figure, now grown somewhat heavy in face and person, sitting at the desk, or restlessly pacing the floor, head down, hands clasped behind his back, forever sniffing at the snuff he did not take, reading letters, dictating replies and messages, keeping his marvelous memory in full play as to methods, details, and men, pleasant of voice, courteous in manner, with but little of the old-time impatience and imperiousness, and in his eyes that tinge of melancholy that even thoughtless Philip had noted ever since the sad day when the Emperor found that his Austrian wife had deserted him, and the son whom he loved so dearly had been stolen from him.

Thus Philip studied him one day, as Napoleon paced the room dictating, advising, commanding. The shapely fingers that were the Emperor's "pride," and which he could often be caught admiring, were dipped again and again into the tortoise-shell snuff-box crowned with the imperial N. Philip stood at the table waiting for a message he was to deliver. The Emperor, laying his snuff-box on the table, turned to consult a letter that bore on the matter in hand. The snuff-box stood invitingly open, and Philip, heedless as ever, could not resist the temptation. With a wink at young Gudin, the Emperor's page, as if to say: "See, you boy! how 'chummy' are the Emperor and I," Philip dipped his fingers into the open snuff-box and took a pinch.

Page Gudin was duly horrified and duly impressed. But, as luck would have it—Philip's usual luck—the Emperor, raising his eyes at just the wrong instant, caught sight of Philip's bold act in the mirror before him. Turning sharply, Napoleon took the snuff-box from the table and with a quick motion thrust it straight toward the mortified Philip.

"Still the same old Philip, eh, you boy?" the Emperor said. "Even the Cross of the Legion has not fully made the page into the man! Here! Keep the box, Captain Desnouettes. It is too small for both of us." And, with a silent laugh at the young fellow's discomfiture, the Emperor went on dictating as if nothing had happened, while Page Gudin had to stuff his shoulder-ribbons into his mouth to keep from laughing aloud, and all the other secretaries exchanged winks and shrugs.

But Philip kept the box.

At last came the June Sunday when, with his old-time ease and affability, as if peace and not war were universal, the Emperor held his final reception in the great gallery of the Louvre.

The whole front of the Tuileries was ablaze with light, and the people coming from the public games that had been given them in the Elysian Fields, cheered the Emperor as he came out to them on the iron balcony of the Clock Tower and watched the display of fireworks.

Philip marveled at the self-possession of the man; he knew how great a host was gathered beyond the frontiers for the Emperor's overthrow, and how soon Napoleon must hasten there to resist and repel invasion.

On the twelfth of June, 1815, Napoleon left Paris for the seat of war. On the fifteenth the French army crossed the river Sambre and fell upon the enemy. Then came Waterloo.

Waterloo!—that famous battle, where Napoleon first met the unconquerable English face to face; where Wellington made his name immortal; that battle glittering in its array, brilliant in its manœuvres, terrible in its intensity, horrible in its loss of life; that battle remarkable for little blunders that led to great results, and magnificent attempts that amounted to nothing; that battle so nearly a defeat for England, so nearly a victory for France, that to this day men cannot see just how it turned the other way, and historians and military writers are even yet disputing as to the responsibility and discussing the operations!

It is not for us to describe nor discuss it here. Napoleon was beaten — conquered, it may be, as the English say, by Wellington; conquered, it may be, as the Germans claim, by Blücher; conquered, it may be, as declares Victor Hugo, the Frenchman, by the will of Heaven, because "for Bonaparte to be the conqueror at Waterloo was not in the law of the nineteenth century. Napoleon had been impeached before the Infinite and his fall was decreed. He had vexed God."

The end of it all—the inexplicable, the unexpected, the impossible, Philip did not see. In his uniform of a special officer of ordonnance, he was in constant attendance on the Emperor, riding here, writing there; now in the saddle, now by the Emperor's side, despatching messages, bearing messages, galloping from point to point, now on the rear of the battle, now in its very front, dodging bullets, dodging charges, restless, active, exultant. He knew from the start that "his Emperor" would win. He heard Napoleon say, making fun of Wellington, "The little Englishman must have his lesson"; he heard him declare of those same English soldiers, "I had rather cut them to pieces than repulse them"; he heard him cry to Ney, "We have ninety chances in a hundred!" His faith in his leader never for an instant wavered.

In all those terrible three days of desperate fighting Philip had been in the thick of it; cutting his way, when need was, through every living obstacle, escaping, with his usual "Philip's luck," the pitiless pelting of that rain of fire and death. He had waved his hat exultantly as the Prussians fell back, defeated, at Ligny; he had watched breathlessly, the stubborn fight at Quatre Bras; he had cheered frantically as his old schoolfellow, big Vieux of the Polytechnic heaved down the door of the farmhouse at Hougoumont that sheltered the English line; he had caught the gleam of victory in the Emperor's eye, as, rising in his stirrups, Napoleon saw Wellington's troops pushed back toward the Soignes Forest. He knew the battle was won.

He saw that never-forgotten figure, now familiar to all the world—the clear-cut profile beneath the plain chapeau, the green uniform of the chasseurs, with its white facings, its broad red sash, and the long gray overcoat, the leather breeches, the high boots, the big white horse with the crimson velvet housings. He heard the quick, brief order to Milhaud's cuirassiers to charge the English on the plains of

"'RIDE LIKE THE WIND TO PARIS. TELL THEM THE BATTLE IS WON.'"

St. Jean; then he caught the voice of the Emperor, satisfied, abrupt, triumphant: "Captain Desnouettes, about! Ride like the wind to Paris! Tell them the battle is won!"

And Philip rode to Paris—eager, flushed, exultant, proud of the news he bore.

Alas! he did not see the end — the splendid charge of those mail-clad squadrons; the terrible tragedy of the sunken road of Ohain; the unyielding stand of the English squares; the repulse; the coming of Blücher; the wild flight; the race with death; the panic; the disgrace; the last charge of the Guard; the heroic stand of that immortal company who died but never surrendered, who, marching on to certain death, never flinched, never faltered, never gave one backward look, but

> Saluting their divinity, erect amid the storm,
> One cry, "Long live the Emperor!" the last their pale lips form.
> Then, with the music on ahead, all passionless and slow,
> And smiling at the English guns, black yawning there below,
> With lifted heads, with flashing eyes, with hearts no fear can tame,
> The Imperial Guard went forward into the furnace flame.

Then they, too, died. Waterloo was won. Napoleon's star had set forever.

Changing horses as he rode, Philip galloped on. He carried his news to Paris. The city heard it with shouts of joy. The young captain, wearied with his desperate ride, reported at headquarters, and then flung himself into the quiet house on the Street of the Fight to rest awhile, and then go out for later tidings of the victory.

Alas! all too soon the tidings came. The courier whom

Philip had passed, riding out as he was galloping in, brought back the sad news that met him on the way. Philip's ride had been in vain. In the early morning, the defeated Emperor came wearily into the courtyard of the little Elysian palace on the Street of St. Honoré, conquered, ruined, overthrown.

But as he stepped from the carriage, and one of his generals said, sadly, "All is lost," Philip, broken with rage and disappointment, saw the Emperor lift his head proudly, and reply in those famous words of an earlier, and, like him, a conquered king of France, "Save honor!"

And Philip felt that even yet there was hope.

CHAPTER XXIII

HOW PHILIP PLAYED THE STOWAWAY

IT was a stubborn fight with Fate that went on in the gilded Elysian palace on the Street of St. Honoré in those bright days of a Paris June. An Emperor was trying the hard task of ruling his own spirit; a conqueror was set to the bitter struggle of conquering himself. Than this there is no harder task in the world, whether for boy or Emperor.

In this fight, allies were not to be depended upon; foes really were friends. For the first would have tempted the overpowered monarch to stand at bay against victorious Europe and mistrusting France; the others were determined to drive him from France at all hazards. And, in his case, to go was his only safety; though had he died fighting for his lost crown, history would have given him even greater glory.

The end came. When his ministers set themselves up to be his masters; when those he had most richly rewarded became his most relentless foes; when France refused to acknowledge as its ruler a man twice "overthrown"; when from those to whom he looked for counsel came only lukewarm loyalty, false protestations, or unwelcome truth; when, from anger at the unreliable Chamber of Deputies, whom he, like Cromwell, threatened to turn out "neck and heels," he would change to indecision, silence, even timidity,— it was plain there was but one thing to do. He did it. On June 22, 1815, Napoleon signed a second abdication, proclaimed his little son, whom Austria had kidnapped, Emperor of the French, and three days after left Paris forever.

He drove to Malmaison, twelve miles from Paris, that beautiful estate, half palace, half villa, which had been the home of the Empress Josephine. Here Napoleon had spent many happy hours in his days of power and prosperity; here Josephine had died while he was at Elba; here the Emperor had planned out his greatest campaigns, his most glorious victories. And here Philip came to him.

Philip could not—he would not—renounce his loyalty, his devotion, his love. There are some natures which are truest when clouds are darkest, and when days are most threatening. Such was that of Philip Desnouettes.

Such, indeed, were yet many of the people of France and the soldiers who had fought for the Emperor; old friends who had shared alike his pomp and his vicissitudes; men and women who had sent their sons to die for France and the Emperor, and would not admit his weakness even when fate seemed so set against him; boys who had been brought up to have faith in Napoleon's glory as in the sun, and would not believe there was such a thing as eclipse.

So Philip, loyal and hopeful still, followed the Emperor to Malmaison. He had almost had a falling-out with Citizen Daunou, because that stanch old republican had favored the removal of Napoleon, and, with Lafayette, had cried for the restoration of the Republic.

Philip cared nothing for a republic. To him, knowing nothing of such a relief from tyranny, a government meant only the Emperor. So here he was at Malmaison, ready to fight for the Emperor—if need be to die with him or for him, so constant was his loyalty, so deep his affection.

"Get me speech with the Emperor, young Desnouettes," a voice said at his elbow, as he was about to enter the palace; "I have something for his good."

Philip turned about. The speaker was Pierre, the inspector of police.

"It is you, Pierre?" Philip exclaimed. "What have you to say?"

"That is for his ear, yonder, my friend," Pierre replied. "Get me speech with him, and quickly. Time presses both him and me."

"So, my boy! it is you?" Napoleon exclaimed as Philip was ushered into his presence. "Ever faithful, eh!" and he embraced the boy warmly.

The Emperor looked worn and "heavy," colorless and sad. Philip was almost startled at the change; but "My faith!" he said to himself, "think what he has gone through! Who would n't look badly after such a strain?" and then he burst out with the feelings that were tugging at his heart.

"I had to come, Sire," he cried. "My place is by your side, if but you will permit me. Use me as you will. See; I am ready. I will work for you; I will follow you; I will die for you. Your enemies are afoot. They plot your ruin. Bid me remain by you. I swear to kill the first traitor who dares to lay hand upon my sovereign."

Napoleon's eyes filled with tears as he listened to the excited boy's pledges of affection. His listlessness gave way to interest.

"Brave boy!" he said. "Were others like you I might yet save France. But no. They are all the slaves of the Allies—those sovereigns of Europe whom once I spared, and who now dishonor themselves in persecuting me. Imbeciles! They would give me up to-day to save France—so they say; to-morrow they will give up France to save their own precious heads. I alone could retrieve all."

Philip fired with enthusiasm. "You can, Sire. You will. Your army is gathering almost within call. It will rally around you. In your soldiers yet remain patriotism and the hope of glory. They are for France and the Emperor. With you to lead them, nothing is to be despaired of."

The Emperor reflected. Already action was becoming a task. "A divided nation and all Europe to face!" he said. "It is too desperate a chance. I dare not plunge France again into war. And yet, we must think of it carefully, my Philip."

Then Philip remembered that Pierre was waiting. He communicated the young inspector's request.

"What! he who is one day to be minister of police?" said the Emperor. "Bid him enter."

Pierre came speedily.

"At great risk I am come, Sire," he said, "for things are not going your way at headquarters. But while a chance remains to aid him who gave me my step, I seize it. I bring you word from friends. I am charged with an offer for safety. See; at Havre awaits an American merchant-vessel; her captain stays for you in Paris. Horses are ready. Everything is prepared. At your orders the captain will sail. To-morrow you may be at sea, safe under the American flag, secure

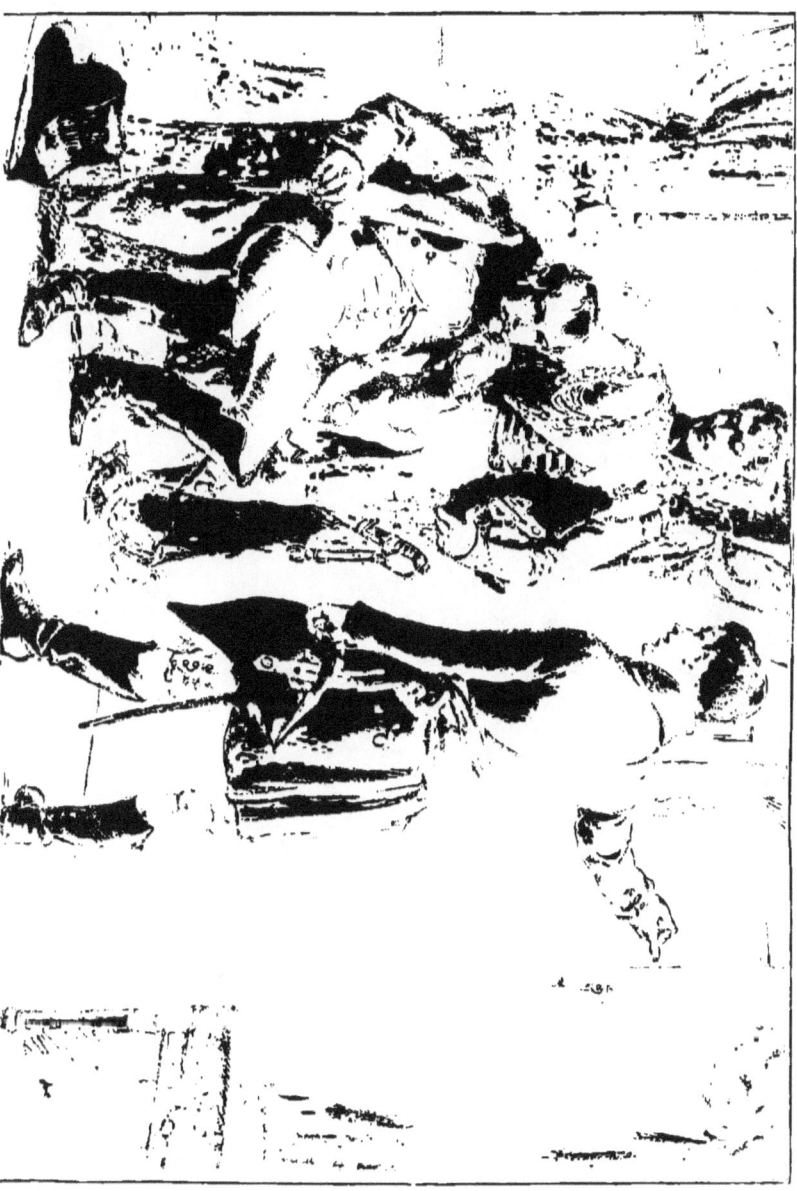

"TO-MORROW YOU MAY BE AT SEA, SAFE UNDER THE AMERICAN FLAG."

from your enemies, free to go wherever you choose. Sire, will you accept?"

Napoleon sat silent. Then he said, "You are a clever one, Monsieur the inspector. And you will swear to me this is not a blind—a plot? I thank you and my friends. It might be well. I could go to America—get some land—be a farmer—end my days in peace. Or, if the land of Washington rejects me, I could go to Mexico; I could lead the Independents there; I might perhaps even found a new Empire of the West. But no," he said, shaking his head; "flight I disdain. It is not for me to skulk in secret from my foes. It is the duty of France to protect me."

Philip, too, was in doubt. He could not bear to think of his hero as flying secretly from France. To him, indeed, France without Napoleon was as day without the sun.

"But, Sire," said Pierre, "reflect! The allies are marching on Paris. They will surround Malmaison. Blücher swears your destruction. At any moment his cavalry can cross the Seine, capture you, and carry you off. Listen! do you hear that? It is the sound of the Prussian cannon." As he spoke the distant boom of cannon fell upon their ears. The enemy was, indeed, at Compiègne.

The guns of his foemen acted upon the Emperor like a tonic. His indecision flamed into action. "The enemy at Compiègne?" he cried. "To-morrow they may be in Paris! It is time to act. Those people at Paris are fools and traitors. Boys, there are a hundred thousand of my soldiers behind the Loire. At their head I can conquer. Here, Philip; write! and you, Monsieur the inspector, deliver the message I would send at once to those waverers at Paris. I may yet save France."

At the Emperor's dictation, Philip wrote rapidly, to the Provisional Government at Paris:

"In abdicating power I have not renounced the noblest right of the citizen—the right of defending my country. The enemy's approach to the capital no longer leaves the least doubt as to their intentions or their bad faith. In these grave circumstances I offer my services as general. I ask to serve France for the last time, and I swear to save it."

"There, Monsieur the inspector," said Napoleon, signing the note, "give this to Caulaincourt. He is my faithful friend. It need not compromise you. Assure him that when the enemy is driven from France I will myself retire. Go."

"And the American vessel, Sire?" queried Pierre.

"It must sail without me. Now it is for us to save France."

Philip caught the Emperor's flash of enthusiasm. He hurried Pierre from the palace.

"But it is to no purpose, my Philip," the inspector said. "Fouché and those others at Paris will listen to no such splendid schemes. Above all else they wish to get the Emperor away and make their peace with the Bourbons. They fear Napoleon; and now that they have him down, they will keep him down. He should have accepted my offer."

Napoleon was pacing his room when Philip returned; he was issuing his orders with his old-time energy. So sure was he of this call from Paris, so filled was he with the idea of action and leadership again, that he dressed himself in his chasseur uniform, called his aides about him, had his horses saddled and in readiness to mount, and waited anxiously for the summons.

He paced the room restlessly. "Why does no answer come?" he cried. "Perhaps Caulaincourt could not arrange it. Captain Desnouettes, go you. Take one of the horses. Hasten to Paris. See Caulaincourt, see Fouché,— any one. Tell them I am ready. Arrange for my coming."

Philip caught the spirit of his master. He was soon riding in haste to Paris. The first official he encountered at the Tuileries was Davout, minister of war — Davout, whom Napoleon had raised from lieutenant to be marshal, duke, and prince of the Empire.

To him Philip told the Emperor's desire. The "butcher of Hamburg," as the Prussians called Davout, fumed with rage.

"You are fools, you and your Emperor!" he cried. "Tell Bonaparte to get out. We do not want him. We have had far too much of him. We can neither fight nor negotiate while he remains. If he thinks he can be chief and master again, he is mightily mistaken. Tell him to get out, to go anywhere—and speedily too, or I will have him arrested, even if I have to grab him by the collar myself."

Philip was almost speechless at such brutal and vindictive words from one of Napoleon's old-time friends and followers. Then he assumed his most dignified bearing.

"Monsieur the marshal," he said, "I have far too much respect for the Emperor and for you to carry such a message."

The war minister turned on him savagely. "Who are you, boy?" he said. "What are you? An officer of France, sir. I am your superior. Get you to the station at Fontainebleau straight and there await my orders."

"Sir," said plucky Philip, "I take orders from no one save my master, the Emperor. I, at least, will not desert

"'I WILL PUNISH YOU FOR THIS!' THE ENRAGED MARSHAL CRIED."

the man to whom others, even more his debtors, deny their oath of loyalty."

"Puppy!" the enraged marshal cried. "Do you hear me? I will punish you for this."

"You shall not. I will give you no chance," Philip returned, quite as hotly. "I resign my commission as captain in the army. I notify you of this, Monsieur the marshal. Henceforth I obey only my honor."

Then, turning, he sprang to his horse and rode to Malmaison, leaving the war minister fuming with rage. And thus Philip threw away his commission.

"What?" cried Napoleon, when, as Philip returned to Malmaison, he read failure in the young man's face. "They do not refuse, do they?"

"They do, Sire," Philip replied, and told of his reception.

At first Napoleon blazed out in wrath. "Arrest me? me? Davout says so?" he cried. Then the reaction came. He flung off his uniform. He sank into a chair. "Well, let him come," he said resignedly. "I am ready, if necessary, to lay my head on the block. I will be a sacrifice for France."

Again he sank into lethargy; again Philip, alarmed for the Emperor's safety, dashed out for news. He feared, lest Davout should carry out his threat. But he learned news even more serious.

"The enemy have surrounded Paris," he reported. "They have almost flanked Malmaison. Blücher swears to take you prisoner, and hang you in sight of the invading armies. It is either fight here, or fly at once. Sire, which shall it be? We can defend you. We will—to the death! But it would be your death, too; for we could not long hold Malmaison against the enemy. Say but the word, though, and here we are, ready to shout, 'For France and the Emperor!' and die defending you."

Again Napoleon started to his feet. He drew his sword.

"Let us defend ourselves, my friends," he cried. " Let us die for France! Alas!" he said, changing from energy to sadness, "it is of no avail. It would be but a useless sacrifice. The people at Paris have no patriotism. They have no energy. All is over. Let us go into exile."

Swiftly the orders were given. The Emperor assumed the citizen's dress. He said good-by to his mother, his brothers, his household, little thinking he would never see them again; and that same evening two carriages drove from Malmaison, carrying Napoleon and his few personal friends to the seacoast, where, at Rochefort, it was said, a French frigate waited to carry the discrowned Emperor to a place of safety.

Philip rode on the coachman's box as in his palmy days of pagedom. He would not desert his hero.

The journey into exile was full of exciting adventures. Wherever he was recognized Napoleon was greeted with the hail that had ever been as incense and inspiration: "Long live the Emperor!" His exile was almost a triumph. Philip felt that if the Emperor would but exhibit his old-time energy and take a determined stand, the return from Elba might be repeated. But it was too late. The old fire smoldered; its flaming-up was only momentary. Napoleon still hoped against hope for a recall to Paris.

At last he reached Rochefort. He had delayed too long. Escape was impossible. The harbor was blockaded by the English fleet.

Then Napoleon, ready with devices and quick with surprises, outdid himself in surprising. " I will board one of the English vessels," he said. " I will throw myself on the hospitality of England. General Gourgaud, you and Captain

Desnouettes shall go to London for me. I will send a request to the Prince Regent."

Protests were unavailing. Napoleon had made up his mind. And then it was that he wrote the famous letter which Lamartine called the appeal of a great soul struggling with the extremities of fate:

ROYAL HIGHNESS: A victim to the factions which divide my country and to the enmity of the great powers of Europe, I have ended my political career, and come, like Themistocles, to sit down beside the hearths of the British people. I place myself under the protection of their laws, which I claim from your Royal Highness, as the most powerful, the most constant, and the most generous of my enemies.

NAPOLEON.

This was the letter which, accompanying General Gourgaud, Philip bore to London. The boy was well-nigh dazed with this unexpected decision of the badgered Emperor. They sailed on a small vessel, which the English permitted to pass the blockade, and were soon in London.

Then Napoleon, bidding adieu to France—to France which had once exulted in him and now cast him out—went on board the English frigate *Bellerophon*,—as guest and not as prisoner,—and sailed for England.

But England feared its dethroned rival too greatly to be magnanimous; it feared him too much to be hospitable. The ministers of the Prince Regent refused Napoleon's request. They had " the Corsican ogre " at last in their power. They would punish and imprison him.

Thus Philip's mission proved a failure, and when, by the side of brave General Gourgaud, he rode into Plymouth, he knew that there was now neither safety, salvation, nor the hope of rescue for his Emperor. Already, he knew, the decree had gone forth that consigned the most marvelous man of modern times, the conqueror of Europe, the terror of England, to a lifelong captivity at St. Helena — that prison-rock across five thousand miles of sea.

Napoleon was transferred to the frigate *Northumberland*. His protest was recorded:

I am not the prisoner, I am the guest of England [he wrote] . . . . I appeal to history. It will say that an enemy, who for twenty years had fought the English people, went of his own accord in the hour of misfortune to seek an asylum under the protection of their laws. What more striking proof could he give of his esteem and confidence? But how did England reply? It pretended to hold out a hospitable hand to this enemy; and, when he had taken it with confidence, England immolated him.

The Emperor's protest was of no avail. England was determined. Napoleon must go.

The farewells were said with all the accompaniment of tears and embraces that are a part of the impulsive French nature. "Farewell, my friends," said the Emperor. "Be happy. My thoughts will never leave you, nor any of those who have served me. Tell France that I pray for her."

But where was Philip? Included among those who had been permitted to come on board the *Northumberland* to say good-by to Napoleon, he had no sooner felt the warm embrace of the Emperor than he had disappeared.

Half-crazed with the defeat of all his high hopes; unable even yet to feel that his Emperor's "star" had set; cast down by the refusal of the English to let him accompany his master into exile; tenderly commanded by Napoleon to go back

"DIVING DOWN INTO THE HOLD."

to his sister and his home in Paris, Philip had taken a sudden and desperate resolve.

What were sister and home to him if this man he had so long served, reverenced, and worshiped was to be consigned to so monstrous a fate? He would go with his Emperor. They should not deny him this.

In the confusion of farewells and departure, while the calm, dignified, and imperial figure of the conqueror was the center of all eyes, Philip had slipped from sight.

Diving down into the hold of the great frigate swiftly and unobserved, the boy hid himself among the orderly array of stores for the voyage that filled the vessel's hold. Good luck—the usual "Philip's luck"—favored his choice of a hiding-place. He had blundered upon a "snuggery," flanked on one side with chests of sea-biscuits and on the other by casks of water. "Now, let them find me if they can," he said. "Good-by, France!"

Philip was bound for St. Helena as a stowaway.

CHAPTER XXIV

THE CITY OF REFUGE

THERE was a reign of terror in France. The King had returned to his own again. The white flag waved over the Tuileries once more; the white cockade was again ostentatiously displayed. The Bourbons ruled in France.

Angry, pitiless, vindictive, the new government—including, alas! many of those who had selfishly deserted the man who had made them—sought to work vengeance on those who had been loyal to him. "The White Terror" ran its course through France.

Not so bloody nor so long continued as that greater and historic "Reign of Terror" it mimicked, the era of prosecution and persecution, which had for its badge the white cockade of the Bourbons, fell upon its victims with assassinations, arrests, and exile. Brave and devoted Frenchmen who had fought and suffered for France, who had contributed to her power, and, by their valor, had secured her glory, were "listed" for punishments and death by those who had been first time-servers and then traitors, or those who had returned from exile hating the man who had made France great.

With a cowardice that was cruelty and a hate that was persecution, France, goaded on by royalists and renegades, murdered its bravest, exiled its best, and created such a feeling of insecurity among those who had supported the plans of Napoleon after his return from Elba that many Bonapartists, or "brigands" as they were now called, went into voluntary exile with the proscribed ones, and deprived France of their services and their ability.

Down the Street of the Fight there came one August day in that sad year of 1815 a well-built young fellow of nineteen, walking bravely, as if confident of a hearty welcome in the house he sought.

The home was reached. It was closed. No answer came to his demand for entrance. No sign of life appeared within or about it. Dazed and distressed the young man regarded that silent house. A hand fell upon his shoulder.

"Philip Desnouettes, brigand and Bonapartist, this is no place for you."

It was Philip, indeed. He looked into the face of his accuser.

"Where are they, Pierre?" he asked anxiously, of the one who had thus accosted him.

"Skipped," was Pierre's laconic reply. "Citizen Daunou was both republican and Bonapartist. The Bourbons do not love him. He was removed from the Archives. He is Keeper no longer. He was listed for proscription. He was wise, and went into hiding before the bloodhounds got upon his trail."

"And Mademoiselle?"

"Gone also."

"But where?"

"Come and see. I have protected them for old time's sake," said the clever inspector of police. "I can protect you—but only long enough for you to leave Paris. You, too, are on the accusing list, my Philip."

Then, through side-streets and by roundabout ways, into the poorer quarters of the town, even to the Street of the Washerwomen, Pierre conducted Philip, and there, in the old house of Mother Thérèse, Philip found his dear ones. They were in hiding — refugees from the absurd "White Terror."

They welcomed joyfully this boy they had almost given up for lost. Mademoiselle clung to him; Citizen Daunou embraced him; Nurse Marcel showered tears upon him; Babette gloried in him; Mother Thérèse patronized him, and Marshal, the big Dane, fawned upon him with the devotion of that most loyal of all animals—the dog.

In the joy at his return even their own hardships and danger were, for the moment, forgotten. From all came the demand for his story.

"It is but a story of failure," Philip confessed.

Then he told them how, when but a few hours at sea, his hiding-place had been discovered by a prying seaman— "Bah! that imbecile," Philip cried, in parenthesis, "what business had he to blunder upon my retreat?"—how he had been dragged out and almost dumped into a passing Dutch hoy—"May it sink forever for having thus been in the way!" he cried again, in indignant parenthesis—without even a chance to be seen by the Emperor.

"But I did get one last glimpse of him, in spite of those rascal English and those imbecile Dutch," Philip said. "It was after I had been flung into the Dutch hoy. We were just casting off from the *Northumberland,* when the Emperor came on deck. In the distance the headland of Cape

La Hague rose dimly through the mist. The Emperor recognized the shore; he knew it was his last look at France. He stretched out both hands toward the misty coast-line as if in farewell. I could hear him plainly as he cried: 'Adieu, land of heroes! Adieu, dear France! A few less traitors, and you would be mistress of the world!' Alas! it was my last sight of his face, my last hearing of his voice. For even as I would have cried out my farewell, those pigs of Dutch hustled me below, and my Emperor was gone from me forever. But not forever; no, not forever! He will yet return to save France. He will yet return to be again the master of the world."

From Amsterdam, to which the Dutch vessel had carried him, Philip said he had made his way into France, hearing of the proscriptions, but never dreaming that he or his would be marked for revenge.

"And now," he said, "what are we to do?"

"What indeed?" Citizen Daunou echoed. Plotting and planning were never the dear old scholar's work, and in the face of his misfortunes he was almost powerless.

"Listen," said clever Pierre, ever ready with devices. "My old chief, the Count Réal, late prefect of police, is one of the 'brigands'—as at headquarters they call all Bonapartists now. He is to go to America. I know his retreat. So, too, do I know that General Lallemand, who is your friend, my Philip, is gathering a company of exiles to sail across the sea to America. Friends there are to arrange for land for a colony. Lallemand and his following will build, somewhere in the western forests, a city of refuge for all Frenchmen in distress; for all driven from their homes;

for all who love Napoleon and sorrow over the fall of France. Why not join them, you?"

"Why not, indeed?" cried Philip, catching gladly at the plan so well suited to his restless nature. "Let us begin life again in a free land. What say you, my sister, will you go? And you, my father?"

"As for me," said Citizen Daunou, "I am an old man, my children. What matter a few years more? Let me die in France."

"As for me," said Mademoiselle, wavering between duty and desire, "what can I say? I would go with you, my Philip. I would stay with you, my father. What shall I do, then?"

Here Babette made so startling a suggestion that Pierre looked at her closely. He had scarcely noticed her before.

"Why not all be White Cockaders?" she said. "It is much easier to give in than to stand out."

Philip caught her by the arm. "What, Babette! you?" he cried, "you whom the Emperor educated?"

Then Mademoiselle followed suit. "What, Babette! you? You to whom the Emperor promised remembrance?"

And Citizen Daunou said, "What, Babette! you? — you a philosopher like Talleyrand and the turncoats?"

Whereupon Babette replied, "But where now is this Emperor with his education and his promises? And Talleyrand remains yet a prince!"

Pierre, the inspector, looked again at this girl with a philosophy.

"Mademoiselle Babette is most sensible," he declared. "She has the wisdom that gets advancement. I gained my

step through the Emperor. But now he is gone; and I—
I am of the White Cockaders. He who turns his coat has yet
a coat to wear."

But Philip could brook no such selfish doctrine. "Better
no coat," he cried, indignantly, "than a turned one. I make
no peace with the Bourbons. They are no true Frenchmen."

"And your Emperor? He was but a Corsican," croaked
Mother Thérèse.

"But the proscribed can make no peace," said Citizen
Daunou. "It is for them only to vanish. My children, I
go with you."

So it was settled. In two days Citizen Daunou, with
Philip, Mademoiselle, and Nurse Marcel, vanished from
Paris, thanks to Pierre's secret help and hasty preparations.
Before the month was out they were crossing the Atlantic,
seeking a home in the new lands of the West.

Many others fled across the sea. By different routes,
landing in different ports, more than a thousand of the best
men and women of France sought refuge in America.

Of these, a certain number—four hundred in all—after
many hardships, after discouragement, privation, disaster, and
shipwreck, finally reached the haven they had selected, and
under the lead of General Lallemand, a brave officer of the
Imperial Guards, and wise old Citizen Daunou, they laid out
and occupied on the banks of the River Trinity, in the province of Texas, their famous City of Refuge.

I should like to tell you the experiences of our friends of
the Street of the Fight as they tried to make for themselves
a new home, amid strange and baffling surroundings. I

could tell you how Philip led an exploring party, and how
he and his companions would have been poisoned, save for
the kindly offices of a friendly Indian; how Mademoiselle
was chased by wild cattle and kidnapped by Spaniards; how
Nurse Marcel almost married an Indian chief; how Citizen Daunou was made vice-president of the military republic, and how Marshal, the big Danish hound, held at bay
twenty Spaniards and Indians, and saved the City of Refuge
from capture and pillage.

But this is all quite another story, and has no bearing on
this tale of the early fortunes of our Boy of the First Empire.

For our Boy of the First Empire became an American
citizen.

"The White Terror" ran its short but sorry course in
France. Valiant soldiers, like Marshal Ney, "the bravest of
the brave," were murdered; patriots, like Citizen Daunou,
were exiled. Finally, reason returned. France was ashamed
of her ungenerous acts. Amnesty was granted, and many of
those who had come to America because they had been faithful to Napoleon, returned at last to the dear old homeland
which, in time, honored and exalted the memory of its most
famous man.

Among those who returned was Citizen Daunou. He
never held office under the Bourbons; but, when he died,
he left behind him the name of a profound scholar, a thoughtful writer, with a memory revered by his countrymen as
that of "one of the purest characters of the Revolution and
the Empire."

As for Pierre, he rose to high honors in the police de-
partment of Paris; and, although he did not reach the goal

prophesied by the Emperor, and become minister of police, he did live to be a chief or prefect. And, yes—he married—whom do you think? Babette. And they were both of them loyal to the white cockade until the tricolor again came in with the Third Napoleon.

Philip and Mademoiselle remained in America. When the Champ d'Asile, or City of Refuge, in Texas, was abandoned because of the demands of Spain, the brother and sister determined to join another French colony, known as "the State of Marengo," in Alabama. But they only got as far as New Orleans. They made many pleasant friends among the French inhabitants of the "Crescent City"—so many, in fact, that Mademoiselle took one of them for life. She married him, and lived and died a lady of New Orleans.

Philip pushed further north. He went into business in Philadelphia, married an American girl, and became a loyal and devoted citizen of his adopted country.

It may not please you to know it; but the fact is, he suffered so much from hearing Americans try to pronounce his unpronounceable name, only to make a terrible mess of it, that at last, in desperation, he determined to change or, at least, to Americanize it.

He looked into the matter, and finding that *des nouettes* meant " tiles," he deliberately took the name of Philip Tyler; and when he became a man, in the famous days of "Tippecanoe and Tyler, too," Philip was often spoken of as "a distant connection of the President."

But, though he learned to look on things differently as he grew older, he never forgot his Emperor. Good American citizen though he became, the stirring experiences of his youth, when he was a frisky page of the palace in the days of the splendid First Empire, were never forgotten by him.

In a small room in his fine Philadelphia home Philip kept what he called his sanctuary. In the center stood a bronze statue of Napoleon, draped with the tricolor and surrounded with trophies of the days that were gone. And not the least interesting of these trophies in his sanctuary were the green and crimson suit of a page of the palace and the light-blue uniform of a lieutenant of ordonnance.

Philip mourned the death of Napoleon; he treasured for years an unquenchable hatred against the jailer England — "perfidious Albion," as he persisted in calling the nation which he also spoke of as the "Emperor's murderer." Though his preference was for a republic, he still did not conceal his joy when, by a questionable method, in the middle years of the century, the Bonaparte power came again to France; when, once more, the tricolor waved over the Tuileries; the eagle and the bees returned; and, at the head of the Second Empire, reigned, as Napoleon the Third, the brother of the same bright little fellow for whom, in days long gone by, Philip had danced "zig-zag" in the great park of St. Cloud, on that never-forgotten June morning when, beneath the chestnuts, the ragged boy of the Street of the Washerwomen first met Uncle Bibiche.

But he did not wait for that day before returning to France. In the year 1840 the world heard great news. England yielded up the dead. Napoleon's body was given back to France.

The desire so ardently expressed in the great Emperor's

will was at last carried out, and, sailing northward from St.
Helena, a French frigate bore to France the ashes of the man
who once held in his shapely hand the destinies of Europe.

Philip hastened to France. With his eldest son, Philip
Daunou Tyler, he stood in Paris that December day when,
with pomp and circumstance, amid tolling bells and booming cannon and marching soldiers, with the tricolor everywhere and through a double row of imperial eagles, the
body of Napoleon was borne to the great Hotel of the Invalids — the splendid Soldiers' Home in the very heart of
Paris, the noble building in which dear old Corporal Peyrolles had lived and died.

Napoleon had conquered. The exile had returned to
France forever. His bones rest at last where he so greatly
desired — " by the banks of the Seine, among the French
people I have loved so well." His glory is that of France.
His fame fills the world.

As a boy and a Frenchman Philip had gloried in his Emperor. As a practical and thoughtful American he learned
to look deeper and to appreciate what Napoleon really was.
That he was a despot Philip acknowledged; that he inflicted
misery and death upon his fellow-men, Philip could not deny.
But that his life was really of value to the world, apart from
its glory and its imperial splendor, Philip also knew. Raised
from the people to save them from themselves when terror
filled the land, Napoleon the Corsican made the France he
served influential, powerful, and progressive. He remade
Europe, shed the light of advancement into Russia, gave to
Germany the idea of national unity that has made her great,
and awoke Italy to the knowledge that she, too, might be an

undivided nation. By his very despotism he advanced the cause of liberty. And since his day the people, learning from his wonderful story their own power and strength, have given the law to kings and the death-blow to tyranny, so that never again shall liberty be throttled by aristocracy nor smothered by the dead weight of a throne.

And to all this Philip felt he had contributed when, amid the splendor of the palace, the gorgeousness of ceremonial and fête, the brilliancy of review, and the smoke and roar of battle, he had lived the life, and done the duty, and seen the sights, and enjoyed the sport of one who exultantly shouted "Long live the Emperor!" as a loyal, vivacious, truthful, happy-go-lucky Boy of the First Empire.

www.ingramcontent.com/pod-product-compliance
Lightning Source LLC
Chambersburg PA
CBHW021201230426
43667CB00006B/496